Care Packages
for the Workplace

LITTLE THINGS YOU CAN DO
TO REGENERATE SPIRIT AT WORK

Barbara A. Glanz

McGraw-Hill
New York • San Francisco • Washington, D.C. • Auckland • Bogotá
Caracas • Lisbon • London • Madrid • Mexico City • Milan
Montreal • New Delhi • San Juan • Singapore
Sydney • Tokyo • Toronto

Library of Congress catalog card number: 96-76231

McGraw-Hill

A Division of The McGraw·Hill Companies

Original artwork on pages xviii, 100, 115, 134, 180, and 186 by Rita Blitt, copyright © 1995.

The author has donated a portion of the proceeds from this book to CARE, the international relief and development agency.

1 2 3 4 5 6 7 8 9 0   DOC/DOC   9 0 1 0 9 8 7 6

ISBN 0-07-024267-4

The sponsoring editor for this book was Richard Narramore, the editing supervisor was Chuck Wahrhaftig of TopDesk Publishers' Group, and the production supervisor was Donald F. Schmidt. It was designed by Judy Allan of TopDesk Publishers' Group and set in Novarese by TopDesk Publishers' Group

Printed and bound by R.R Donnelley & Sons Company

McGraw-Hill books are available at special quantity discounts to use as premiums and sales promotions, or for use in corporate training programs. For more information, please write to the Director of Special Sales, McGraw-Hill , 11 West 19th Street, New York, NY 10011. Or contact your local bookstore.

 This book is printed on recycled, acid-free paper containing a minimum of 50% recycled de-inked fiber.

Praise for *CARE PACKAGES FOR THE WORKPLACE*

To my God, whose light I hope shines through this book, to my mother, who all through her life has given me her special CARE packages®, and to all the beautiful friends I've been blessed to work with all over the world who have taught me so much about what it means to care.

® CARE Packages is a trademark of CARE, the world's largest private relief and development organization. This year, CARE is celebrating its 50th anniversary.

CONTENTS

VII   R = REASON FOR BEING   133

VIII   E = EMPATHY   157

FOREWORD

Recently I was asked to talk about the workplace on the noon news in one of our major cities. I arrived at the radio station just before noon but didn't get on the broadcast until about ten to one. When I finally got to speak to the newscaster I said to him, "Didn't anything good happen in this town today?"

He looked surprised and said, "What do you mean?"

I replied, "I've been sitting here for fifty minutes listening to your news and all I heard was bad news about robberies, about accidents, about rape, about O. J. Simpson, about everything going on here and elsewhere that seems to be negative. Surely something good has happened here today."

My comments caught my reporter friend off guard. And yet, I feel so strongly that today in every way we seem to be accenting the negative. Good news seems to be lost. I'm not just talking about happenings in cities and countries around the world; I'm talking about organizations too. Where is the emphasis today when it comes to managing people? Is it on catching people doing things right or wrong? Whenever I ask that question people are quick to admit that the accent is on the negative. We have to do something about that trend.

In *The One Minute Manager*, Spencer Johnson and I talked about catching people doing things right and it hit a nerve in this country. Well, let me tell you, Barbara Glanz and *Care Packages for the Workplace* is going to hit nerves all over the place. This is a marvelous book and Barbara Glanz is a marvelous human being. What does she want to do? She wants to generate in our workplaces the spirit of hope, caring, a personal sense of meaning, and even fun. Barbara thinks this is a must if organizations are to survive today and so do I. Why? Because most organizations are running on fear. People fear for their jobs, they fear they are going to do something wrong and get lambasted for it; it's just not fun being in most organizations today. While evaluation of performance is necessary, it does not have to be a punitive process. In fact it should be the very opposite. It should be an important part of coaching in helping people perform.

Dave Barlo, one of the most thoughtful teachers and consultants I've ever met, gave me the best expression of that philosophy. He got interested in the training of whales. One day he asked some of his training friends at Sea World in Florida where they actually trained the whales if they used some of the coaching techniques that he and I have been talking about for years. They said, "Yes, with one addition." Before they attempted to train a new whale to do anything, the trainers told David, "We feed them and make sure they're not hungry. Then we jump in the water and play with them until we've convinced them that we mean them no harm." That's a powerful statement. That's all about trust, isn't it?

If you want to create a different work environment, *Care Packages for the Workplace* is perfect. Barbara Glanz will uplift you with the many ways you can reach out and help others be their best. With the ideas she has gathered from positive work environments she has visited, this book will be motivating and enlightening. Barbara wants to jar you into really looking at what's happening in your place of work and to give you a new understanding that *you* can make a difference. You can make a difference in the moment-to-moment choices you make in your interactions with others. In the midst of all the confusion and chaos that seems to surround the world today, there is hope, and Barbara Glanz and her wonderful book is the ultimate care package for you. C.A.R.E. stands for creative communication, atmosphere, respect, and empathy—all things we need more of in organizations today.

Thanks, Barbara, for writing this book. I know you, the reader, will enjoy it. Barbara Glanz cares about you, she cares about organizations, she cares about life. Let her be your guide for making a difference in your world.

Ken Blanchard
Co-author of *The One Minute Manager*

PREFACE

I recently read the following quotation: "Our souls are leaking. We are in a recession and we are receding." I believe that most people in corporate America as well as in other workplaces in our world today are surrounded by fear, distrust, insecurity, change, and confusion. There is a lack of hope and a lack of caring.

This sense of isolation and fear has led to an alarming state in our country: eight out of ten high-school students are freely admitting that they cheat in their schoolwork, the population has little trust left even in our country's highest leaders, and when interviewed, most people said they would do almost anything (lie, cheat, disparage others) in order to keep their jobs. Dr. Jean Houston, Director of the Foundation for Mind Research, in a speech titled "Design and the Possible Human Being," tells of a recent study in Japan in which a million people were polled regarding what they felt were the major problems of today. The number one answer was a sense of meaninglessness and spiritual aridity.

A long-term, highly paid sales person in a large and well-respected institution recently told me of his feelings about work. Each day he leaves the office feeling insignificant and humiliated. Management is accomplished through fear and threats. There is no trust for anyone and no respect for individual differences, skills, or experience. The only thing that is valued is power and money. In his words, "Each day they extract their pound of flesh!" You can imagine the atmosphere of this organization. And sadly, I believe this description fits many places of work in the 90s.

The 70s and 80s were characterized as the "ME" generations. Stephen Covey describes how people in the last 40 to 50 years have begun to rely on the SELF—stressing personality characteristics and self-improvement techniques to better their lives rather than relying on character and principles that reach far beyond the self and become anchors for behavior.

I believe that when we go into our selves, we function out of *fear* (Am I good enough? Will they like me? Will I say the right thing? What ulterior motives does she have? What if I don't do this well?).

And when we go outside of our selves, we function out of *caring*, focusing on another person and his or her needs, and that is how we can add more spirit to our workplaces. We must come back to the anchors of character and principles that Covey so powerfully presents. Each chapter of this book will give you specific skills and tools to help you put your energy into caring rather than into fearing.

The purpose of this book is to jar people's thinking into *really* looking at what is happening in their places of work and to give them a new understanding that THEY CAN MAKE A DIFFERENCE. They can make a difference in the way they treat each individual they encounter in a day's time. In the midst of all the confusion, change, fear, and hopelessness, THERE IS HOPE! The hope comes from the understanding that even though I may not have control of the forces surrounding me, I will ALWAYS have control over my interactions with each person I encounter, one on one.

My desire with this book is to provide the understanding, the motivation, and real-life, specific "how-to" ideas that anyone can apply in his or her job to make a difference. Spirit begins with one person and spreads like the aura of a lovely smell or taste, permeating the atmosphere until the whole is enveloped in an uplifting, joyous experience. This phenomenon can occur in your organization and mine. The hope is in each individual spirit reaching out to others.

I have used the metaphor of "C.A.R.E. Packages®," familiar to many of you, which originated during World War Two. These were packages of food and clothing that were sent to needy people overseas during the fighting. For many victims of the war, these packages became a means of survival. They also represented a way for those folks left at home in the states to contribute, to make a difference, even though they were not a part of the "action." Even today, we refer to packages we send to our children who are away or in college as "C.A.R.E." packages, and in my own experience, many times these gifts of love and caring were just what I needed to make it through a tough time.

Yes, our souls are leaking; yet as we begin to send C.A.R.E. packages to one another both inside and outside our places of work, there will be a regeneration of spirit. It becomes exponential—as you care for others, they will, in turn, have more spirit to care for someone else. No matter what level of the organization in which you function, you are, just like the folks at home during the war, a part of the action—you can make the choice to care, one on one, no matter what is going on around you.

The main text of this book will consist of concrete ideas of ways you can extend the C.A.R.E. metaphor, symbolizing the elements of a spirited workplace, in your own individual choices at work:

C   stands for "Creative Communication"

A   stands for "Atmosphere" and "Appreciation for All"

R   stands for "Respect" and "Reason for Being"

E   stands for "Empathy" and "Enthusiasm"

My hope is that my spirit and the spirits of so many others who have contributed to this book will transfuse and inspire your spirit to reach out to others in a new and caring way despite the circumstances which surround you. As we change our behavior in those one on one interactions, so will the spirits of our organizations change. And that will, in turn, change the fear, hopelessness, and confusion into a new sense of the integrity of each person we encounter and the choices we have to make a difference. We can then be free to do our best work, to enjoy and appreciate others, and to feel a true sense of our worth and value. And, in the process, our organizations, as well as the individuals within them, will thrive.

Barbara Glanz
Barbara Glanz Communications, Inc.
4047 Howard Avenue
Western Springs, Illinois 60558
708-246-8594
708-246-5123 (fax)

ACKNOWLEDGMENTS

Never believe that a few caring people can't change the world. For indeed, that's all who ever have.

—Margaret Mead

This is a book of the heart! The beautiful, caring spirits of all the people who have contributed in some way shine throughout this manuscript. They are special gifts to our world. I thank and cherish them for the difference they are making in big ways and small:

Richard Narramore, my editor, who has been my cheerleader, barrier-breaker, and above all, a believer in the message of this book. He even has his own special story in the Appreciation chapter! He has many times called this "an unorthodox" book, so I give him special gratitude for putting up with all the creative ideas I have had throughout the process. Thank you, Richard, for CARING about me and this book!

To Ken Blanchard, my very special friend, teacher, and spiritual companion. How I love his stories! Thank you, Ken, for a foreword that touches our hearts.

To my dear friend, Rita Blitt, for the drawings from her heart created just for this manuscript. To Joel Goodman, Hyler Bracey, and Bob Nelson, all people with spirit and heart, who took special time to write about their passions just for you and me. And to Bill McAlpine for his delightful cartoons. To Mark Banus, Mike Hall, and Bonnie Michaels, who continued throughout my writing to give me new resources and ideas. Thank you all for caring!

And most of all, to my patient husband, Charlie, who put up with all the extra work and inconvenience of my being unavailable nearly every minute I was not on the road speaking. Thank you, honey, for being there in so many special ways.

And to all of you whose stories are in the book, thank you for the difference you are making in the world. It has been a blessing to work with you and to share your contributions to creating more caring places to work.

Regenerating Spirit

The movement towards regenerating spirit in the workplace is an attempt to create a sense of meaning and purpose at work and a connection between the company and its people.

"WHAT IS SPIRIT IN THE WORKPLACE?"

> *Spirit does not need to be "'brought into" an organization. Spirit already lies within virtually every employee. It is waiting to be released and provided with a hospitable and nurturing environment—policies, structures and systems, behaviors, norms, and habits to support what people prefer: a place to work that feeds their spirit and produces a fine and worthy product or service.*
>
> —MARIE MORGAN
> *"Spirit in the Workplace" At Work, Sept./Oct. 1993*

The Situation in Our World Today—The Need for a Regeneration of Spirit in the Workplace

Is your organization experiencing downsizing, re-engineering, overwhelming changes in technology and job descriptions, debilitating stress, lack of trust, low employee morale, and a "dog eat dog" atmosphere? If so, then you need this book!

"It's thrilling to watch them first thing in the morning, ready for the kill."

As I speak and consult in organizations all over the world, I see employees who are depressed, confused, fearful for their jobs, stressed by having to do more with less, and overwrought from constant change. There is a lack of hope and a lack of caring.

In a Roper poll published in March of last year, they found that employee morale and job satisfaction was at the lowest point it has ever been *since Roper began doing the poll decades ago.*[1] Last year *USA Today* reported that 42 percent of American workers felt "used up" by the end of the day.[2] Consider this story from a July 25, 1994, article in *Fortune* titled "Burned-out Bosses":

A director of marketing reflects with contempt and exhaustion on the reorganization that the television station she works for has gone through. When she joined the company in 1985, she respected her employer and enjoyed managing her staff of eight. Two years ago a handful of senior executives unexpectedly revealed plans for a top-to-bottom restructuring. She says, "I walked in one day last summer and discovered I had three full-time jobs. With a load that size, I hate them all. As a result, my employer is getting 10% of my former creativity and maybe 50% of my energy. I'm the classic employee who quit but still shows up to pick up her paycheck."[3]

In a January 19, 1995, article "Downsizing moral: Morale needs a lift" by Ronald E. Yates in the *Chicago Tribune*, a survey found that revitalizing the workforce was becoming the No. 1 priority of human resource directors. Forty-one percent of those responding said that was their top priority in 1995. "The fact that companies have elevated this concern to the top of the list says a lot about the state of the American workplace," said Walter L. Polsky, chairman and chief executive of Chicago-based Cambridge Human Resource Group, Inc., which conducted the survey.

> **We live in a vastly complex society which has been able to provide us with a multitude of material things, and this is good, but people are beginning to suspect that we have paid a high spiritual price for our plenty.**
>
> **—EUELL GIBBONS**

I believe that in the last eight to ten years many organizations, because of their commitment to quality, have spent so much time and money focusing on systems and processes that they've forgotten their most important resource, PEOPLE. I recently heard of a senior manager's statement, "We hired workers and human beings came instead!"

I think we MUST regenerate in our workplaces the spirits of creativity, hope, caring, a personal sense of meaning, and even fun for our organizations to survive. We *know* that happy employees are more productive employees, and as a new spirit permeates the atmosphere, profits, too, will increase. This regeneration must begin with each individual, and in the next chapters of the book I am going to give you some ideas to help make this happen in *your* organization. Throughout this book we will focus on the CHOICES you each have to make a difference in your workplace.

In the past, Leadership has been hierarchical, based on power, with each person trying to please the person above him or her. Today I believe that leadership is in a state of CHAOS with so many things changing in the workplace that everyone is trying to learn how to best survive. However, just as winter turns to spring, so does chaos lead to regeneration.

> **Work can provide the opportunity for spiritual and personal, as well as financial, growth. If it doesn't, then we're wasting far too much of our lives on it.**
>
> —JAMES A. AUTRY
> *Love and Profit—The Art of Caring Leadership*

What must happen, I think, for the future of our organizations is that we must move to a new level of SELF-MANAGEMENT in our workplaces where each employee, no matter what level in the organization, takes personal responsibility to make a difference by adding more respect and caring to his or her place of work. In Chapter Two you will learn how you can use the acronym C.A.R.E. to help that happen.

When each of us fully understands the CHOICES we have to make a difference, we will no longer need to see ourselves as "victims," and we can leave with a new sense of purpose and commitment to one another and to our very important jobs.

What Spirit in the Workplace "Looks Like"

Spirit in the workplace often begins with one person and spreads throughout the organization. Let me tell you a story about one spirited workplace I encountered at a Wyndham Hotel in Houston, Texas:

> I travel a lot in my work of speaking and writing, and one of the things I dislike about this part of my job is eating alone. It always makes me feel lonely to see others laughing and talking, and sometimes I have the uncomfortable feeling that I

look like I am waiting to be "picked up" by someone! So, I usually order room service for several nights to avoid that discomfort. However, sooner or later, I feel as if I need to get out of the room. At this point my strategy has become to go down to the nice restaurant the moment it opens because then it is not very crowded, and I don't feel as uncomfortable.

After having room service three nights in a row, I needed to get out. Although the nicer restaurant opened at 6:30, I arrived at 6:25. The maitre d' met me at the front and made a comment about my "really being there early." I responded by explaining my dislike of eating alone in restaurants. He then took me back and seated me at a lovely table.

He returned to the front of the restaurant for a few minutes; however, he soon returned to my table and said, "You know I am all caught up with my work, and people don't usually start coming to our restaurant until after seven o'clock. You said you didn't like to eat alone, so I wondered if you'd mind if I sat down with you for a while." I was delighted! He shared with me information about his career goals, his hobbies, and lots of the dilemmas of balancing a restaurant career with having a family and the difficulty of being at work on nights, weekends, and holidays. He even took out pictures of his children, his wife, and his dog! After about 15 minutes had passed, we noticed some customers at the front desk, so he excused himself. However, I noticed out of the corner of my eye that before he went to the front, he stopped out in the kitchen for a few moments.

He then proceeded to seat the arriving party. About that time, out of the kitchen came one of the waiters. He walked over to my table and began to talk with me. He said, "My station is way in the back tonight, and I'm sure no one will be seated there for awhile. I'm not really busy. Do you mind if I sit down with you for awhile?" Again, I was delighted to have some company. He shared with me what his career goals were and what his life was like—he was working two different jobs and going to school as well as trying to maintain a relationship with a girlfriend! We had a wonderful chat until someone was seated in his station and he needed to excuse himself.

Soon after he left, out came one of the young busboys, and he, too, asked if he could sit down with me for a few minutes. He hardly spoke any English, but I had taught English as a Second Language, so we had great fun talking about his experiences in coming to America. What he shared with me were all the expressions they had taught him in the kitchen when he first arrived in this country! As the restaurant got busier, he finally excused himself to attend to his work. Before I had left that night, however, the chef even came out of the kitchen and sat down with me for a few minutes!

When I asked for my check (about 1½ hours later), there was an almost audible pause in the restaurant. All of the people who had sat down with me came over in a big group to my table. They presented me with a long-stemmed red rose and said, "This was the nicest night we've ever had in our restaurant." And I cried! What had begun as a lonely night had ended as a beautiful experience—for both employees AND customer.[4]

THAT is spirit in the workplace! Can you imagine how much fun they must have had peeking out the hole in the kitchen door, asking each other, "Who's up next?" It was almost like a relay team! They made me feel special, they told me about themselves and their lives, they gave me their free time, and they even did something extra at the end. And in the process, they had fun, too. The spirit began with the Maitre d' who took the time to really listen, not just to my business need to eat but to my human need to not feel lonely, and spread throughout the restaurant from the individual to the team. This can happen in your organization, too. Let's look at some ways to do it.

Notes

1. Gerstner, John. 1994. "Good Communication, Bad Morale." IABC Communication World, March, pp. 18–21.

2. Paxton, Loryn. 1994. "Foregoing the American dream." Chicago Tribune, Section 1, Saturday, 17 September, p. 21.

3. Berlin, Rosalind Klein. 1994. "Burned-out Bosses." *Fortune*, 25 July, pp. 44–52.

4. Glanz, Barbara A. 1994. *Building Customer Loyalty: How YOU Can Keep Customers Returning*. Burr Ridge, IL: Irwin Professional Publishing, pp. 89–91.

II

"HOW TO C.A.R.E. ABOUT YOUR WORKPLACE"

The hard stuff is easy,
The soft stuff is hard.
And the soft stuff is a lot more important
than the hard stuff.

—MILLIKEN & COMPANY

A Framework for Understanding Spirit in the Workplace

This book is all about CHOICES—the choices you have to make a difference no matter where you work, what your job is, how much change is going on around you, what your boss is doing, or what your co-workers believe. In every individual interaction you have, you have some awesome choices, and only YOU can decide whether they will be positive or negative.

Joseph Epstein in *Ambition: The Secret Passion* writes:

> We do not choose to be born. We do not choose our parents. We do not choose our historical epoch, or the country of our birth, or the immediate circumstances of our upbringing. We do not, most of us, choose to die; nor do we choose the time or conditions of our death. But within all the realm of choicelessness we do choose how we shall live: courageously or in cowardice, honorably or dishonorably, with purpose or in drift. We decide what is important and what is trivial in life. We decide that what makes us significant is either what we do or what we refuse to do. But no matter how indifferent the universe may be to our choices and decisions, these choices and decisions are ours to make. We decide. We choose. And as we decide and choose, so are our lives formed.[1]

Choice #1—The Three Column Chart: Your Choice in Any Interaction

I am a very visual person—I need to SEE the choices I have in a concrete form, so several years ago I created this three column chart that helps me truly understand the difference I can make in each interaction I have with anyone.

> **The choice we offer people is what creates accountability.**
>
> **—PETER BLOCK**
> *Stewardship—Choosing Service Over Self-Interest*

I can discount that person, making him or her feel less important than me or my organization. That is a "minus." If I just take care of the business at hand, I have left that person with a "0" or a neutral experience. However, in every single interaction, I have the opportunity to choose to make a human-level connection, recognizing that person as a unique human being, thus leaving them with a "plus" experience. They are a little happier because they interacted with me.

A quotation from Mother Teresa has become a philosophy of life for me, exemplifying this chart:

> Be kind and merciful. Let no one ever come to you without coming away better and happier.

Please make a copy of the three column chart and keep it with you for one week. Each time you interact with anyone, put a check

Discount (-)	Business Only (0)	Human Level Connection (+)

Your Choice with Every Interaction

mark in the appropriate column, evaluating what kind of an experience you created for that person. At the end of the week if you have more checks in the "+" column, you have not only contributed to creating a more positive spirit in your organization, but you have made the world a little better. Celebrate yourself! You have made a difference.

Choice #2—The Two Levels of Every Interaction

Another important choice we have is to recognize that there are two levels to any interaction whether it is written, electronic, or face to face. There is the Business level, which is all about getting the business done, the project or task at hand, generally the purpose for the interaction to occur. And there is also the Human level, which is all about how the participant FEELS about the interaction.

How often in our world today do we only interact on the business level, leaving people feeling cold, unimportant, and invisible? While the Business level is related to productivity and profit or the bottom line, the Human level makes an impact on a person's morale, sense of self-esteem, and purpose.

> **When love and skill work together, expect a masterpiece.**
>
> **—C. READE**

**Your Choice with
Every Interaction**

Notice that an interaction is not "whole" unless both levels are fulfilled.

As you think about this model, think about going to the doctor. How many doctors have you been to who treated you only on the *Business* level? How did you *feel* about that interaction? Also, think about managers you have had. Have you ever been managed by someone who managed you only on the *Business* level? Did you do your best work for this person? As you think about all your interactions, become aware of the choice you have to make a difference by always considering the Human level.

In a spirited workplace, both managers and employees interact on both the Human and the Business levels, and they choose to create positive experiences for one another.

Choice #3—What People Want from Their Jobs

A fascinating study first conducted in 1946 asked a thousand employees to list ten common workplace rewards in order of their motivational impact. The employees' supervisors were then asked what they thought their employees' list would look like. The supervisors' guesses were overwhelmingly wrong.

What is most interesting to me about this study is:

1. How little supervisors REALLY understand their employees.

2. How little actual control they have of the things they THINK their employees want (good wages, job security, promotion and growth in the organization).

What Employees Want

Employees	Supervisors
1. Interesting work	1. Good wages
2. **Full appreciation of work done**	2. Job security
3. Feeling of being in on things	3. Promotion and growth in the organization
4. Job security	4. Good working conditions
5. Good wages	5. Interesting work
6. Promotion and growth in the organization	6. Personal loyalty to employees
7. Good working conditions	7. Tactful discipline
8. Personal loyalty to employees	8. **Full appreciation of work done**
9. Tactful discipline	9. Sympathetic help with personal problems
10. Sympathetic help with personal problems	10. Feeling of being in on things

Copyright 1995, Kenneth A. Kovach. *Reprinted by permission of John Wiley & Sons, Inc.* [2]

> **3.** How MUCH control they have of the things employees actually want (interesting work, full appreciation of work done, and a feeling of being in on things).
>
> 4. This study was conducted in 1946, 1981, and 1995. Each time, there was no change in the supervisors' false perception that being appreciated is relatively unimportant to employees.

Again, we see some of the choices we have as leaders in our organizations if we want to motivate our employees to do their best work. Motivated employees create a spirited workplace!

The Acronym C.A.R.E.—the Elements of a Spirited Workplace

As I have studied, written, and spoken about this topic which is so deeply a part of my personal mission, I have found several elements that exist in all the spirited workplaces I have studied. These elements, many of which are based on principles and values, make up the acronym C.A.R.E. and become the objectives for a spirited workplace:

C = Creative Communication

A = Atmosphere and Appreciation for All

R = Respect and Reason for Being

E = Empathy and Enthusiasm

As we think about the three top things employees want, "Interesting work" involves creativity, empathy, and a reason for being; "Full appreciation of work done" reflects enthusiasm, atmosphere, and appreciation for all; A "feeling of being in on things" is related to creative communication and respect. The elements of a spirited workplace *are* the things all employees want in their jobs.

Also consider how these elements exemplify much more of the Human level than the Business. They are all about our *feelings* toward our work. Therefore, a spirited workplace involves the *whole* person, allowing them to function fully on both the Business and the Human levels. As your organization and the individuals within it begin to C.A.R.E. about one another in even more visible and creative ways, a new spirit of commitment and hope will emerge.

How to Use this Book

All of the ideas in this book are being used by real people in real organizations. Some of them involve individual actions, others are more specifically for leaders in the organization, and still others are activities for a whole department or work team. Keep an open mind as you read through them. Let these ideas trigger for you things that you might do at work tomorrow to make a difference.

If you work in a bureaucratic culture or have a grouchy boss, don't give up! You will read about some of the creative, fun things that even government organizations, such as the Michigan Department of State, are doing to regenerate spirit in their offices. Force yourself to stretch and try new things, to get out of your comfort zone. Remember the old adage, "It's easier to get forgiveness than permission." In most cases spirit begins with one individual and spreads throughout an organization. So, YOU can be the one to begin the caring and help rekindle lots of inner lights.

One of my personal missions in writing this book is to give credit to those organizations and individuals who are truly doing things to regenerate spirit in their places of work. If you, your organization, or others that you know of are doing exciting things, please let me know for future editions of the book.

> I never look at the masses as my responsibility.
> I look at the individual.
> I can only love one person at a time.
> I can only feed one person at a time.
> Just one, one, one. . . .
> So you begin . . . . I begin.
> I picked up one person—
> Maybe if I didn't pick up that one person,
> I wouldn't have picked up 42,000.
> The whole work is only a drop in the ocean.
> But if I didn't put the drop in,
> The ocean would be one drop less.
> Same thing for you,
> Same thing in your family,
> Same thing in your business.
> Wherever you go
> Just begin . . . one, one, one.

Mother Teresa
Words to Love By

Notes

1. Epstein, Joseph. 1980. *Ambition: The Secret Passion*. New York, NY: E.P. Dutton.

2. Kovach, Kenneth A. 1995. "Employee Motivation: Addressing a Crucial Factor in Your Organization's Performance." *Employment Relations Today* Vol. 22, No. 2. New York, NY: Wiley & Sons, Inc. or Wiley-Liss, Inc.

III

C = CREATIVE COMMUNICATION

Amidst the massive outpouring of data, computer printouts, and television's tasteless wasteland, people are starving for authentic, caring human communication for the workforce.

RICHARD S. RUCH AND RONALD GOODMAN
Image at the Top

"Surprise Your Receivers: They *Will* Get the Message!"

Are you bombarded by stacks of paper, inundated by E-mail messages, and spending half your life in unproductive meetings? Do you find that even with all this flood of "information," things are happening in your organization and you are sometimes the last to know?

You are not alone! Consider these interesting facts shared by Dr. Arthur DeKruyter on communication: 60 percent of the individuals in the United States are in some form of the information business and the average North American worker spends over 50 hours a week communicating in some way.[1] When a large publishing firm polled over 500,000 subscribers regarding the most serious business problem existing today, the overwhelming number one answer was "Communication."

In a study reported in *Business Week* May 1994 and the *Wall Street Journal* August 1994 by the Council of Communication Management on how 705 employees at 70 companies felt about company communication, they learned that

- 64 percent don't believe what management says.

- 61 percent don't feel well-informed about company plans.

- 54 percent feel that decisions are not explained well.[2]

For many organizations, communication has become a deep rut full of dreary memos, dismal meetings, and negative feedback. The result is unhappy, uninformed, or bored employees and ultimately poor customer service and lowered productivity.

One of the most crucial elements of a spirited workplace, I believe, is communication—and not just "ordinary" communication. The more creatively a message is sent, the greater the chances that the message will be noticed and heeded amidst the overwhelming clutter of communications that surround us. So, my challenge to you is to get out of your boring cocoon of routine business communications. Become aware of all the marvelous, innovative, and creative ideas you can use to assure that *your* message gets heard, and you will not only improve the spirit in your workplace, but you will also have fun doing it!

Whenever you send a communication, whether it is written, electronic, or face to face, ask yourself three questions:

> **Personally, I would sooner have written Alice in Wonderland than the whole Encyclopedia Britannica.**
>
> **STEPHEN LEACOCK**

1. Does it get the information across *clearly and accurately*? (This is the Business level and the purpose for the communication).

2. How does it make the receiver *feel*? (This is the Human level and includes the choice of words, the tone, and the sincerity of the sender).

3. Will it *surprise* the receiver? (This is the element of creativity that is so important in a spirited workplace).

Have some fun as you communicate creatively with others. Harvey MacKay, the author of *Swim with the Sharks Without Being Eaten Alive*, told the National Speaker's Association at its 1995 annual conference in Minneapolis, Minnesota, of one delightful way he got his audience's attention. He was asked to speak to a very large group of managers of Schick, the razor blade company. After he was introduced, he came out with bandaids all over his face. His opening line was, "I *knew* I shouldn't have bought that Gillette razor!"

> **Creativity is to see what everybody else has seen, and to think what nobody else has thought.**
>
> **ALBERT SZENT-GYORGYI**

It is also important in a spirited workplace to communicate to ALL employees in an authentic, open, caring way. Here are some suggestions from John Gerstner, the manager of internal communications for Deere & Company, Davenport, Iowa, about how to do that:

Be creative.

Be honest.

Be human.

Be reassuring.

Be enthusiastic.[3]

You simply cannot communicate enough. Experts say that you have to tell the average adult something six times before it is internalized. The challenge becomes communicating a message in such a creative way that it only has to be told once! A spirited workplace is filled with people who are fully utilizing all their creative energy to implement the three levels of any communication, and they are having a great time.

Using Signage

THE IDEA:

One way to get people's attention and to surprise and delight both customers and employees is to use creative signs. They not only add fun and spirit to the workplace, but they can also indirectly share the values of the organization.

THE IDEA IN ACTION:

 Stevinson Jaguar in Denver, Colorado, has placed a sign in front of visitor parking spots:

> *Some of the nicest people in the world*
> *park here and become our customers.*

 Harrah's casino on the riverboat in Joliet, Illinois, has an employee van that reads:

> **THIS BUS CARRIES PRECIOUS CARGO**

 Peterson's Ice Cream Store in Oak Park, Illinois, has a sign posted in its entrance area:

> *All children allowed to roam free in*
> *this store will be captured and used as*
> *slaves!*

 The Marriott Hotel in Auckland, New Zealand, has a sign on the outside door of the employee entrance and loading dock:

> *The greatest people in the world work*
> *here*

 The Limited Credit Services has hung yellow and black "Yield" signs from the ceiling of its telephone customer service area that say:

> **QUIET! Reps Listening**

A computer hardware firm uses the following sign on the cover of their company brochure:

In driving to Lansing, Michigan, last week, we noticed the following creative use of signs:

> In a construction zone, the first sign announcing "Construction for the next 8 miles," had a bright yellow sign posted on the top with a frowning smile face. At the 4 and 6 mile signs, the frown became less and less. At the next sign which read, "Construction 2 more miles," the smile face was neutral (a straight line for the mouth), and at the last sign, "End of construction," there was a great big smile on the added yellow sign!

 Karen Profita, an account representative with Our Lady of the Lake Regional Medical Center in Baton Rouge, Louisiana, a frequent traveler like myself, always checks under the bed on her way out of the hotel to make sure she hasn't left anything. On one trip she says that when she got down to look, in the middle of the floor underneath the bed was a little sign that said, "I've looked here, too!" signed by the maid.

 When I was Manager of Training at Kaset International, a customer service training firm, we had many people who were bothered by interruptions when they had a looming deadline on work, so we created the following sign:

Oooohhh Noooo!
I'm really in a time crunch
and could use your help!

 and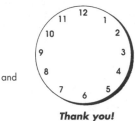

Please interupt ONLY for customers and
other very important matters between...

Thank you!

 Saint Francis Medical Center in Peoria, Illinois, began a campaign called "Share the Vision" to promote their new vision for the future of the center. Part of that campaign was a series of Vision Watch signs:

Remember the great Burma Shave signs that used to dot the landscape? From 1927 to 1963 they were safety reminders and subtle ads for shaving cream. A series of five or six signs spaced several yards apart along a highway delivered a short message. One early example was:

His tenor voice
She thought divine
'Til whiskers scratched
Sweet Adeline
Burma Shave.

Or these from 1962:

Ben met Anna
Made a hit.
Neglected beard
Ben-Anna split
Burma Shave.

Passing cars
When you can't see
May get you
A glimpse
Of eternity
Burma Shave.

To help us see the dimensions of the Saint Francis Vision, a series of Vision Watch signs will be appearing in the walkways connecting the Gerlach and Glen Oak Buildings. If you have some ideas for catchy rhymes, let PR or Marketing know.

The Burma Shave/Vision Watch signs were a great success and later these sign frames were made available to publicize other programs in the hospital.

Marianne Kosits, a consulting instructor at IBM's Advanced Business Institute in Palisades, New York, tells of a sign in her veterinarian's office:

> **The doctor will be with you in a moment. Sit. Stay.**

TIPS FOR IMPLEMENTATION:

Get people throughout the organization involved in thinking of creative ways to communicate through signs. For example, look at the signs you have posted throughout your building now (both inside and out) and see how you might convey the same message in a more gentle, fun, creative way.

Creative Invitations

THE IDEA:

If you are inviting employees or co-workers to a function of some sort, be creative in the way you issue your invitation.

THE IDEA IN ACTION:

Diane Carden, a senior training consultant and owner of Daystar Productions in Lutz, Florida, uses small 3-D items glued on neon post cards as reminders for training classes. One card had small plastic ants glued on it and the caption was, "Training classes can be a picnic. Come and find out why!" Another had a small plastic sandal glued to it and it read, "Kick off your shoes and come to... "Another had a small clock attached and said, "Don't waste your time getting here for the best class ever!" Each card was placed on the participant's desk the day before with the class, room number, and date written on the back. These cards with other attachments and captions could also be used as a follow-up to classes.

> **Creativity may express itself in one's dealings with children, in making love, in carrying on a business, in formulating physical theory, in painting a picture.**
>
> **JEROME BRUNER**

This is a different kind of creative "invitation": Marianne Kosits shared that when her father's business has trouble collecting a bill, they write on the invoice, "We've carried you for 10 months. If you think about it, that's longer than your mother carried you. Please remit." It makes customers smile AND it gets the bill paid!

Di Anne Barron-Binder, an Assistant Vice President of United National Bank in Vienna, West Virginia, prints out posters and banners advertising various events at the bank. She then gives them to employees to take home to have their children color. A thank-you article is printed in the company newsletter with the child's name, and each "artist" receives a small gift from the bank. She ends up with creative invitations, and the employees and their children love it!

> **The only real antidote to fear is COMMUNICATION.**
>
> **CHRIS LEE**
> *"Return of the 'Tingler'"*
> *TRAINING Magazine*

TIPS FOR IMPLEMENTATION:

No matter what the function is, try to have a theme. Then come up with a creative way to use that theme to get people's attention and make them want to attend. Party shops and dollar stores are excellent resources for ideas. Anytime you can include a food treat or anything three-dimensional you will *immediately* capture their interest!

Creative Ads

THE IDEA:

In order to get your customers' or employees' attention, you must surprise them. Encouraging creativity in the advertisements you use will add a new spirit of "thinking outside the box" in your organization.

THE IDEA IN ACTION:

Enterprise Systems in Wheeling, Illinois, is the leading provider of operational information systems software for the Healthcare Industry. One of their ads reads:

We *Encourage* Nurses *to* SWIPE T*he Supplies*

This certainly gets people's attention through a play on words. They mean to "swipe" the item over the scanner: *"Rest assured, it's entirely legal. With the new TouchScan™ Point-of-Use Resource Management System, the simple act of swiping bar coded supplies across a scanner becomes a revolutionary movement for nursing and supply management."*

Artist's Frame Service in Chicago, Illinois, uses "shock value" in their ad:

We Don't Want any Satisfied Customers

We think that being satisfied is fine . . . when you pick up your dry cleaning or get your car washed. But at Artist's Frame Service, we want you to be THRILLED. Anything less would be a shame.

Red Lion Hotels & Inns has a creative ad featuring a picture of a newborn baby wrapped in a blanket which can be humorously taken two ways:

We're Beaming With Pride At How Far Our Night Clerk Went With a Guest.

They then go on to tell the story of Orlando Perez. He was a front desk clerk who talked a woman through her delivery at home while they were trying to find her husband who was attending a conference in the Vancouver, Washington, hotel. They go on: *Don't expect this particular service at all Red Lion hotels. But do expect us to go surprisingly far out of our way for you.*

National Public Radio's "Performance Today"® ad uses the following headline for an upcoming symphony performance:

> **We'd Like To Thank All The Nagging Mothers Who've Made These Performances Possible.**

This one especially got my attention because I was one of those nagging mothers!

TIPS FOR IMPLEMENTATION:

As your employees are challenged to create ads that are fun and attention-getting, even if they are only for posting in the company washrooms, they will transfer that creative spirit to other aspects of their jobs.

Creative Promotions for Company Events

THE IDEA:

The more creatively you advertise and promote a company event, the more likely you are to have good attendance. When you capture people's attention, they *want* to find out what the event is all about!

THE IDEA IN ACTION:

When one of their local department stores went out of business, Charlene Eshleman, Manager of Staff Development for the Foreign Mission Board in Richmond, Virginia, bought a mannequin that she lovingly named "Sadie." The first time Sadie appeared on the scene was after some downsizing had occurred in the organization. Dressed as a stressed-out woman, she made her debut in the lobby of the building to advertise a workshop called "Diminishing Stress Through Laughter." She was missing a button, her slip was showing, her lunch bag was leaking, her shoe was untied, her nail polish was chipped, and it was definitely a bad hair day! Charlene found that the employees immediately identified with her and began to make even more changes. They unzipped her skirt, turned her belt around, and simply used her as a catharsis for all of their stress. From then on, Sadie became a company legend!

> **All the companies that are alive are realizing that they need more creative, vital, and adaptable workers.**
>
> **DAVID WHYTE**
> *The Heart Aroused: Poetry and Preservation of the Soul in Corporate America*

When they held a workshop for professional women, Sadie became the model of professional dress and held a sign advertising the day. To promote a communications program, Sadie held a cartoon bubble that said, "What's going on?" And when I was asked to speak to the whole company on "Send a C.A.R.E. Package—Regenerate the Spirit in Your Organization," Sadie became a cheerleader complete with pompoms!

Charlene also uses a cardboard cutout of Einstein as an attention-getter. To advertise another course, he held a sign that said, "You don't have to be an Einstein to learn Speed Writing!"

> **I speak Spanish to God, Italian to women, French to men, and German to my horse!**
>
> **EMPEROR CHARLES V**

TIPS FOR IMPLEMENTATION:

Think of unusual ways to get your employees' attention as you advertise and promote company events. You might even bring in volunteer entertainers that relate to the theme. Try different things, but it is especially fun to have a company mascot or legend, such as Sadie.

Be Creative in Giving Directions

THE IDEA:

Whenever you can give someone directions in a creative way, they will be much more likely to read and follow them.

THE IDEA IN ACTION:

A friend recently gave me a copy of the owner's manual for a Giro bicycle helmet. It begins with these words:

> **Read These Warnings or You'll be Sorry**

1. This helmet is intended only for bicycling. Do not take it motorcycling, riding mopeds, or SCUBA diving.

2. Do not have a wreck. If you do have a wreck, discontinue using this helmet until we have inspected it to make sure there isn't any invisible damage. We mean it! You may not be able to tell when your helmet's sacrificed its life in order to save yours.

3. No helmet—not even those iron gladiator things they wore in Ben Hur—can protect the wearer against all foreseeable impacts.

Other headings in the manual are:

> **How to Make Your Helmet Fit Like Your Own Hair**
>
> **What to Do if You Crash**
>
> **What Do the Lawyers Have to Say?**

(Reprinted courtesy of Giro Sport Design, Inc., Soqual, CA)

This is the first owner's manual I've ever seen that is FUN to read!

TIPS FOR IMPLEMENTATION:

You can apply this idea to any kind of instructions or directions you might need to give. Have fun with them! You will not only get your receiver's attention and add a smile to his or her perhaps otherwise dreary day, but you will also ensure that the directions really do get *read*.

Give Creative "Excuse" Notes

THE IDEA:

Especially when your organization goofs and causes an inconvenience for a customer, a note of excuse may be in order and certainly creates wonderful, positive PR in the final analysis.

THE IDEA IN ACTION:

According to a January 1, 1995, article in the "For Starters" section of the Sunday magazine of the *Chicago Tribune* newspaper, the Metra transportation system in Chicago, Illinois, gives out "Train Delay Notices" when the customer's train is unavoidably late. A journalism instructor tells of a student walking into his class 45 minutes late who handed him a piece of paper that said, "To Whom It May Concern: This is to advise that Metra trains were unavoidably delayed due to difficulties . . . We apologize for any inconvenience."

Metra spokesperson Susan Kemp says, "We call them notes to the teacher. You give them to your employer so they don't think you slept late." Metra began giving out the notes two years ago, and they are given whenever one of the 3,763 trains that Metra runs weekly are more than 10 minutes late.[4]

TIPS FOR IMPLEMENTATION:

When might you or your organization cause an inconvenience for a customer or an employee? This kind of creative communication makes everyone feel better—the employee and the customer!

Have a Creative Newsletter

THE IDEA:

Remember that the only way to get your customers' attention is to do something a little bit different. Because we are all bombarded with paper, a newsletter will only be read if it surprises or delights your customers.

THE IDEA IN ACTION:

PressScription, a direct mail marketing company for printers, in Orlando, Florida, creates delightful newsletters for their printing customers. The slogan on one issue, printed in a child's handwriting, is "We Never Kid Around When it Comes to Your Business Printing."

Some of their other monthly themes have been: Mark Twain, with the slogan, "Full Steam Ahead"; Dreams, with information on dream analysis, a darling little bedtime character as a graphic, and the slogan "We make your dreams come true"; "Words to the Wise," with all kinds of facts about industry words, acronyms, and even tips on word usage; and even Angels, with a column on "Earn your wings," encouraging readers to do random acts of kindness and a graphic for "You made my day!" notepads. One of the owners of PressScriptions, Diane Dahlquist, said, "You can take ANYTHING and make a theme out of it." Get those creative juices going—you will delight your readers!

TIPS FOR IMPLEMENTATION:

Pick a theme and create your newsletter around it each month. Make sure it is an attention-grabber!

Enclose a Surprise in Your Mailings

THE IDEA:

Whenever you send something to someone, whether an internal or an external customer, you will really get their attention if you enclose a surprise.

THE IDEA IN ACTION:

 Jim Macanowicz, the president of Crazy Diamond Productions, a video production company in Lindenhurst, Illinois, recently sent me a copy of a promo video he had made to demonstrate his expertise. In the package with the video, he included a bag of microwave popcorn and a bag of Raisinets with a note saying, "Pop the popcorn, open the candy, and sit back and enjoy my video." I did just that!

 A graphic artist with whom I work always sticks a piece of sugarless gum in everything he sends whether it is work he's done for me, a bill, or even an ad. I NEVER throw anything from him away unopened!

Another company puts a bag of M&M's with a note that says "Thanks for your business" in every package they mail to customers. Their packages never ever sit on the loading dock!

If possible, enclose something memorable that ties in with your product, service, or job. Or you might want to make this your personal signature, like the graphic artist, and always include the same thing. Even putting a "signature" sticker on everything you send captures people's attention.

Spice Up Your Memos and Other Communications

THE IDEA:

Anything you can do to creatively jazz up the memos and communications you send will result in more people actually reading them.

THE IDEA IN ACTION:

A senior manager decided how he would get his employees' attention. Whenever he sends a memo that has unpopular news (not terrible news, but things he knows the employees won't like very much), *he staples a kleenex to the memo!* This has caused more fun in the workplace and has allowed everyone to "lighten up."

What does your fax cover sheet look like? Most of them are terribly boring, and a wonderful opportunity to communicate creatively has been lost. Consider adding a favorite quotation, a graphic, a cartoon about your industry, or even a fun thought such as "Only _____ shopping days until Christmas!"

Henry Tanners, who calls himself the "Chief Worker" of Chaos Unlimited in Smithtown, New York, really gets his receiver's atten-

Chaos Unlimited

We're on the cutting edge
20 Hill Lane, Smithtown, New York 11787
1-516-360-0998   Fax 1-516-265-3598

There ain't nuttin' we won't put on a button"!

Cows give more milk when they listen to music.

The Mona Lisa has no eyelids.

Beethoven was 5"2.

It's illegal to have a pet pig in Iceland.

Little Known Fax

TO: _____

FAX NUMBER: (   ) _____-_____

FROM: <u>Henry Tanners, C.W. (Chief Worker)</u>

NUMBER OF PAGES: _____ <u>including cover.</u>

DATE: _____ / / _____

SUBJECT: _____

_____

_____

tion with his fax cover sheets titled "Little Known Fax." He even has several different ones for different occasions.

TIPS FOR IMPLEMENTATION:

Get your creative juices going to think of things you can add to make your communications more fun and palatable. Get out of your mental locks and TRY SOMETHING NEW!

Use Photos in Memos and Letters

THE IDEA:

Add a photo to your memos and letters to personalize them and create a relationship. Today many of us have access to the technology to do this easily.

THE IDEA IN ACTION:

Michelle Prescott of Enterprise Systems in Wheeling, Illinois, told me about how she scans photographs onto her memos and letters.

> If you remember, I mentioned how I use photos in memos and letters that I send to my clients. This is a sample with a picture of me and my family. If it's just a short note, I'll print out a page with just the photos and then handwrite a note. I also use this for personal correspondence as well, to hopefully let my creditors, insurance company, etc., know that there is a person on the other end! I know that there are photo business cards, so perhaps one day photo memos will be the rage.

Concepts Direct of Longmont, Colorado, pioneered the idea of using photographs on address labels. Customers can even send in their own photograph to be reproduced so the receiver will know exactly what the sender looks like!

TIPS FOR IMPLEMENTATION:

Since we are almost all in the business of building relationships, what a wonderful way to become "real" to the people with whom we communicate! If you have children, you can constantly update coworkers with their pictures on your memos. If you have gone on a vacation or have had a special event in your family, that could be the photo you use. Or you might include a photo of your team or department, your building, or your community on a memo or letter to an external customer. If you talk to people only on the telephone and may never have a chance to meet face-to-face, a picture certainly will enhance the relationship, especially since so many of us are visual. You can even scan a photo onto the envelope! This becomes a very special way to add a truly personal touch to one's job, thus generating a new spirit of commitment.

Find Ways to Jazz Up Your Meetings

THE IDEA:

Most organizations are plagued with long, tedious meetings. Get your creative juices going to come up with some fun ways to add sparkle to otherwise boring get-togethers.

THE IDEA IN ACTION:

Peggy Moczul of the Department of Civil Service in the State of Michigan tells about what she and a colleague did to liven up their meetings:

> Paul Perla and I were asked to facilitate a session for a committee that was evaluating three contract proposals. Each of the eight committee members was asked to vote "yes" or "no" on 30 evaluation questions for each of the three proposals, constituting 90 votes from each member. The meeting was scheduled for all day and was anticipated to be less than exciting!
>
> As facilitators, Paul and I decided to make the meeting as interesting and active as possible. We developed a voting tool we hoped would hook people's interest and help speed the voting process. We went to the party store and purchased red, green, and yellow plastic luncheon plates. We then stuck the red and green plates together and glued a tongue depres-

sor between the two plates as a handle. When they arrived at the meeting, committee members were asked to hold up the green plate for a "yes" vote and the red plate to vote "no." We even gave them a yellow plate to flash if they had a question prior to voting.

The committee members loved the creativity, and people could hardly wait to vote! The day-long meeting was completed in four hours.

 Ron McKinley, the former Vice President of Human Resources for APAC in Cedar Rapids, Iowa, utilizes participative meeting concepts in his weekly staff meetings. As the "person in charge," he does not run the meetings but uses the experience as a team-building exercise for his staff. Every week the positions change, and these positions are voluntary so that everyone gets to be everything! These are the positions to be filled for each meeting:

LEADER   This person runs the meeting, gathers agenda items, and assigns a time to each. He/she may choose where and how the meeting will occur. One week they may meet outside; another they might all sit on the floor; and another time the leader may choose to have them all wear party hats or even stand up, just to keep them surprised!

FACILITATOR   This person is in charge of the process, making sure that the group stays on the subject and that all have a chance to speak.

SCRIBE   This member takes notes and produces the minutes. (Ron told me that this was his job for next week's meeting.)

MATH PERSON   This person is asked to bring a calculator, and whenever statistics or figures are needed, he/she will do the required math.

FOOD PERSON   This staff member brings some kind of treat to the meetings.

Ron's meetings are fun because there are weekly surprises, the staff is encouraged to be creative, which impacts their other work, and everyone participates in all the roles, so there is a genuine feeling of equality. In fact, several of his staffers have told me that they now ENJOY meetings!

TIPS FOR IMPLEMENTATION:

Challenge yourself to try something new and creative each time you are in charge of a meeting. If you surprise participants, they will actually look forward to coming to your meetings, and you will be surprised at how much more work you will get accomplished.

Educate All Employees about Your Business

THE IDEA:

Give employees small bits of information about the business that they may not know. Then not only will they feel more pride in the organization as a whole and better understand their role in the overall process, but they can also help to educate your customers.

THE IDEA IN ACTION:

 Condell Medical Center in Libertyville, Illinois, has created "Don't Keep It a Secret" cards that they use internally to promote their services. They are delivered with employee paychecks every other week. In addition, they have poster size versions throughout the hospital, and the information is covered again in each newsletter.

Cynthia Schleich, RRT, Community Liaison, says: "The program stems from an effort to educate our staff so that they will do 'word of mouth' advertising. Our facilities have grown so quickly in a short amount of time that it is difficult for everyone to know all about Condell. So we are providing specific points of information in the hopes that our employees will learn and pass it on."

TIPS FOR IMPLEMENTATION:

Try messages on paychecks or paycheck envelopes, "Did You Know . . . " with interesting facts about your company. Include a littleknown or new piece of information each week when employees turn on their computers. Have trivia contests using questions about your organization. Any time you educate your employees about your business, you are creating ambassadors for your organization. It is fun to share new information, particularly when you are involved in some small way.

Help People Learn

THE IDEA:

Find different and convenient ways to help your employees stay current in their field.

THE IDEA IN ACTION:

Dimitris Tsitos of Athens, Greece, introduced into Mobil Oil Hellas a system called FEM, "Our Friendly Communications." They sent audiocassette tapes to their traveling front-line personnel, mainly marketing representatives, which had classical music designed to boost morale and enhance adult learning on one side and a marketing or sales speech by an expert on the other side. To encourage them to listen to the speech, they always asked for their comments and suggestions. Also, once a year each marketing representative was asked to give a short speech on what he/she had learned from the tapes. He said the employees appreciated this easy way to learn and develop themselves.

TIPS FOR IMPLEMENTATION:

With more and more people spending time in their cars or on their computers, using appropriate technology can maximize employees' time and create "painless" learning experiences.

Have Fun with Stickers

THE IDEA:

Every one loves stickers! They remind us of our childhood, and they are an inexpensive way to make people smile.

THE IDEA IN ACTION:

After training Michigan Department of State employees in "Building a Customer-Oriented Organization," I got a call from one of the clerks in a branch office. The day after the training, she went to the store and bought lots of gold stars. Now, when someone passes their driver's test, she puts a gold star on it. The customers are delighted!

Don Law, an Insurance Recruiter for APAC Corporation, always carries little yellow sticky dots with him. As he walks by the stations of the telephone service representatives, he draws all kinds of faces on them (mostly happy ones) and sticks them on their telephones. The TSRs can't wait for him to come to their station!

The *Chicago Tribune* newspaper in its Tempo section on August 8, 1995, ran a story by T. J. Becker titled "Tattoo you—Return-address labels let people put pizzazz in their postal personalities." The article is interspersed with pictures of many different return-address labels, and they write, "Whether you're a devoted fan, a nature buff, or a perfect angel, there's an address label to tell people where you're coming from. . . . More than a mere convenience, today's address labels have become a tattoo of sorts, allowing individuals to rise above a sea of anonymity."

There are labels for collectors (antique cars, Barbies, teddy bears, angels), animal lovers, musicians, sports fans, artists, gardeners, environmentalists; labels with city skylines, cartoon characters, and even Elvis! Labels can make a political statement or support a cause, or they can be a representation of what the person loves and how the person perceives himself/herself. Some folks use labels that support Mothers Against Drunk Driving or UNICEF. A person who uses a label of her Scottish terrier says she can't imagine what life would be like without a dog, while another zealous gardener wants a label with gourds on it! One design can be used exclusively, or they can be changed according to the occasion. For example, one person loves Warner cartoon characters. She uses Tweety Bird for family and friends but the Tasmanian Devil for bills!

> Every morning I get up and look through the Forbes list of the richest people in America. If I'm not there, I go to work.
>
> ROBERT ORBEN
> *Former speech writer for Gerald Ford*

TIPS FOR IMPLEMENTATION:

Stickers are an inexpensive way to add creativity and fun to your workplace. Stickers that affirm and appreciate others are always fun—we can never be told "good job" enough times. You might also want to consider using stickers or address labels that represent something your company does—book address labels for publishing companies, bandaid labels for a doctor's office or hospital, telephones for telecommunication companies, money labels for financial institutions. Remember the only way to stay in people's memory is to get their attention!

Defrost Management-Employee Communications

THE IDEA:

Use new, creative ways to communicate with employees that encourage open and honest feedback. A recent survey by the Families and Work Institute showed that employees value open communication between managers and workers more than any other organizational attribute. In a federal commission finding reported in an article titled "'Distrust and animosity' on job" in the June 3, 1994, issue of the *Chicago Tribune*, as many as 50 million workers would like a voice in on-the-job decision-making but are not given the chance. Finding and implementing ways for management to communicate more openly with employees will greatly impact the spirit in any workplace.

THE IDEA IN ACTION:

At Armstrong Machine Works, a division of Armstrong International, either the general manager or the controller hands out employee's paychecks every week, whether they work in the office or in the shop. To do this, the GM or controller must know all the names of over 300 employees. Why do they do this? In his book *Managing by Storying Around*, David Armstrong says, "We want everybody to have a chance to be heard. While we have an open door policy, not everybody feels comfortable walking into the corner office. By having an officer of the company hand out paychecks, everyone is assured that at least once a week, he'll have a chance to ask a question, voice a concern, or suggest an idea to one of the people in charge."[5]

Several organizations I have worked with have what they call "Grapevine sessions" to stop the flow of the rumor mill and to help create more open communication throughout the organization. The company-wide understanding is that any employee can call a grapevine session at any time that he or she feels there are too many rumblings, rumors, and concerns going on simply by going to the president or another officer of the company and requesting it. On that same day, all employees who are able are asked to gather in a large area of the company, and the president, or whatever company officer is available, addresses their questions and concerns in an informal way. Some organizations schedule these informal communication meetings on a regular basis. Often they are followed by a relaxing, social time sponsored by the company, with the group sharing snacks and a soft drink, and the discussion continues in a more relaxed setting.

One of the keys to the success of these sessions working is the commitment by the company officers to be completely open and honest. Even when they can't give specific information, they CAN honestly explain why and when they will be able to share certain information. Another issue of vital importance in larger organizations is to include offsite personnel by either audio taping or videotaping these sessions and then sending out tapes within 24 hours.

It is best to set limits to these meetings—no more than 45 minutes to one hour, and to determine an organizational Code of Conduct as to what behaviors are acceptable in these meetings. These grapevine sessions can be implemented in departments or divisions or throughout the whole organization.

Kenneth Smith, the General Manager of the O'Hare Hilton Hotel in Chicago, Illinois, has a "Meet the Manager" meeting once a month. These informal meetings are held in a neutral room at different times, and he encourages open, off-the-record discussions of whatever the employees would like to talk about. Ken always shares his philosophy that the *employee* has the most important job in the company, and his job is least important. This level of communication and respect has won his hotel the award for the outstanding airport hotel in the country! Ken also sends a birthday card to each employee on his or her special day.

> **Intellectual strategies alone will not motivate people. You must have people's hearts to inspire the hard work required to realize a vision.**
>
> JOHN NAISBITT AND
> PATRICIA ABURDENE

To better improve communication between him and his employees, a senior manager decided to give each of his direct reports five paper silhouettes of his hand for Christmas each year. Each paper "Helping Hand" represents one hour of his time that the employees can choose to use any way they want during the year. Not only do they have lots of fun teasing him about baby-sitting, mowing their lawns, or walking their dogs, but as he actually does the tasks they choose, such as sorting and delivering mail, answering telephones, entering data, and manning the front desk, he not only learns more about them and their work, but he also creates a new spirit of teamwork and communication.

Notes

1. Glanz, Barbara A. 1993. *The Creative Communicator: 399 Tools to Communicate Commitment without Boring People to Death!* Burr Ridge, IL: Irwin Professional Publishing.

2. Valencia, Alis, & Sumberg, Mary Lou. 1994. "DisTrust." At Work, Vol. 3, No. 3, May/June, p. 16.

3. Gerstner, John. 1994. "Good Communication, Bad Morale." IABC Communication World, March, pp. 18–21.

4. Lyon, Jeff. 1995. "Ma Metra." Chicago Tribune, "For Starters" section, Chicago Tribune Sunday Magazine, 1 January.

5. Armstrong, David. 1992. Managing by Storying Around: A New Method of Leadership. New York, NY: Doubleday Currency.

6. Glanz, Barbara A. 1993. The Creative Communicator: 399 Tools to Communicate Commitment without Boring People to Death! Burr Ridge, IL: Irwin Professional Publishing.

Personal Action Ideas

Write your ideas here!

IV

A = ATMOSPHERE

In environments in which human needs are acknowledged and talent and creativity are allowed to flourish, employees give their all.

CHARLES GARFIELD
"Creating Successful Partnerships with Employees"
At Work, May June 1992

"Serious Fun: The Necessity of Play at Work"

One of the most important elements of a spirited workplace is an atmosphere that makes people feel good about coming to work. People want to work in an environment in which they feel cared for and respected, they can have fun, and their creative spirits are encouraged.

In his audiotape series *Embracing Chaos*, Tom Peters admonishes us to "FIGHT BLAND DULLNESS!" So, it is important to create an atmosphere that is alive and full of vitality, a happy place to be.

Look at the physical surroundings—your lobby, the cafeteria, the hallways, your office. Tom Peters says that if your hallways are boring, chances are everything about your organization is boring, including your product or service!

In an article called "Fun at Work" in the May/June 1994 issue of *At Work* magazine, author Ann McGee-Cooper says:

> Intense pressure brings a shift in the body's neuropeptides, which can lead to feelings of exhaustion, depression, and just plain dullness. A deep belly laugh stimulates the brain to produce endorphins. Endorphins renew you physically, mentally, and emotionally; they contribute to feelings of relaxation and refreshment, as well as a positive outlook.

Experts say that the most productive workplaces have at least 10 minutes of laughter every hour. How is your workplace doing? Remember the choices you have to make a difference, and begin to add some fun and creativity to the place where you work.

My friend, Joel Goodman, the Director of The HUMOR Project in Saratoga Springs, New York, and the author of the book *Laffirmations: 1001 Ways to Add Humor to Your Life and Work*, is the expert on creating an atmosphere of fun and creativity. I asked him to share some of his ideas on this subject:

Invest in Jest: Take Your Job Seriously and Yourself Lightly

Most people value humor personally and yet may question its use in the serious world of business. This is due to a variety of mythconceptions—let's take them one at a time:

Mythconception #1: People won't take me seriously if I use humor in my leadership role.

It *is* important that we take our jobs seriously. . . and it is also important that we take ourselves lightly. In the words of Don Seibert, former chief executive officer and chairman of the board of the JCPenney Company:

"The most senior people and virtually all of the chief executive officers with whom I'm personally acquainted have highly developed senses of humor. Humor is a common thread I've seen in thousands of meetings in different companies on the most serious of subjects. Humor helps you to keep your head clear when you're dealing in highly technical information or difficult decisions where choices aren't that clear."

In other words, you can be a serious professional without being a solemn professional.

Mythconception #2: Humor is not serious: The bottom line takes precedence over the funny line.

In fact, the two lines can go together.

1) *Jest for the health of it!* William Fry, Jr., M.D., who has done research on the physiology of laughter for over forty years, lends support to the notion that laughter is like "internal jogging." Humor can have an impact on individual health . . . and collectively on corporate health. Cents of humor might save dollars . . . for individuals and organizations!

2) *"Stress" and "burn-out"* have become household words in the 1990s. A report to the President's Science Advisor places the cost of stress to the economy at $200 billion annually. Humor can be a powerful antidote to stress—it can help us to move from a "grim and bear it" mentality to a "grin and share it" orientation.

This shows up over the long haul, too. In his longitudinal study of what made for "success" in Harvard College graduates, Dr. George Vaillant found humor to be one of *the* key mature coping mechanisms that insured that stress didn't kill more quickly and commonly. In other words, you can use humor to add years to your life and life to your years.

Mythconception #3: To be humorous, you have to be a joke-teller.

Although joke-telling is one way to transmit humor, it's not the only way. There are thousands of ways to invite smiles and laughter in addition to joke-telling So, if joke-telling is not your forte or if it is inappropriate for you to become the stand-up comic on-the-job, then there are alternatives. Here are four tips to get you going:

1) *Inject humor appropriately into memos and meetings*—for instance, when facing a confusing issue or seemingly hopeless dilemma, using one of Woody Allen's tongue-in-cheek quotes might shed lightness and perspective: "More than any other time in history, humankind faces a crossroads. One path leads to despair and utter hopelessness. The other, to total extinction. Let us

pray we have the wisdom to choose correctly."

2) *Use humor as a tool rather than as a weapon.* Laughing with others builds confidence, brings people together, and pokes fun at our common dilemmas. Laughing at others destroys confidence, destroys teamwork, and singles out individuals or groups as the "butt."

3) *Build humor into the corporate culture.* There are a growing number of bottom-line-successful corporations that have been practicing what I've been teaching. Southwest Airlines' President Herb Kelleher is well-known for his creative sh'nanigans and modeling of humor from the top down. Kodak also "got the picture" by setting up a "Humor Room" as a strategy to inspire creativity and innovation. Ben & Jerry's has established a "Joy Committee." They offer "Joy Grants" to their employees who have an idea that will bring more joy into the workplace.

4) *Humor's Bottom Line.* I love a quote I came across from Tom Peters: "The number one premise of business is that it need not be boring or dull. It ought to be fun. If it's not fun, you're wasting your life." Set the tone by modeling your ability to take your job seriously and yourself lightly.

Humor is a delightful and powerful way to open doors, minds, and hearts. Isn't that what our organizations should be doing?

Dr. Joel Goodman

Part One

THE CORPORATE ATMOSPHERE: IT DOESN'T HAVE TO FEEL STIFLING

The "Whine" Cellar

THE IDEA:

Every organization needs a "fun" place for people to go to unwind, to get their spirits renewed, and to simply "let their hair down!" Find an unused space of some kind in your building and create a unique spot for this renewal to happen.

THE IDEA IN ACTION:

After I had spoken to a large organization about the idea of creating an atmosphere conducive to fun and revitalization, they called to tell me what they had done. A group of people in one department spontaneously got together, found an unused office space, stayed late one night, and decorated it all in black. When the other employees arrived the next morning, they were greeted with a banner over the entrance to the unused office, which read "THE WHINE CELLAR." People began to bring in stress toys, cartoon books, stuffed animals for those who needed a hug, and even coloring books. This spot became the favorite gathering place not just for the folks who were having a bad day, but for the whole company. And remember—What is the favorite social event of chronic complainers? A whine and cheese party!

> From an employee standpoint, a great place to work is one in which you trust the people you work for, have pride in what you do, and enjoy the people you are working with.
>
> **ROBERT LEVERING**
> *A Great Place to Work*

> There's no reason that work has to be suffused with seriousness...Professionalism can be worn lightly. Fun is a stimulant to people. They enjoy their work more and work more productively.
>
> **HERB KELLEHER**
> *CEO, Southwest Airlines*

TIPS FOR IMPLEMENTATION:

This is an idea that can be adapted to wherever you are physically working. It could be located in a cubicle, an unused closet, or even a corner of the breakout room. It is just important to be considerate of the people working near the area, so if it is in the midst of a work area, perhaps make it a "quiet" room with beautiful, relaxing posters on the walls and inspiring books of quotations to read. It is always best to locate the space where it won't disturb the work of others, and if it can be somewhat removed from the normal workspaces, it will truly seem like a "getaway!"

Burn the Barriers

THE IDEA:

One very concrete way to allow people to "let go" of negatives and focus on the positives is to physically get rid of them, especially when many of these barriers involve things that have happened in the past.

THE IDEA IN ACTION:

 I recently worked with the training team in the Switching Systems Division of Rockwell International, in Downers Grove, Illinois. The team had been without a leader for over a year and had had several acting managers who could only devote part of their attention to the team. In that time, the team had nearly disintegrated, and although the individuals were doing a good job of training their customers, personality conflicts and negative feelings were the norm when it came to the team as a whole.

We spent the first day together focusing on their *individual* roles in regenerating the spirit in their workplace, and the second day we spent focusing on coming together as a *team*. In one of the early exercises, we listed all the barriers that were keeping them from being a strong, cohesive team and posted these on the wall of the room. By the end of the day, the group had created their own code of conduct and had worked through many of the issues they had earlier listed as barriers.

As a closing for the day, we took all the barriers listed, went out in the parking lot where the Manager of Education Services and the Director of Division Marketing had a portable grill going, and *burned the barriers*! We then made S'Mores (An old Girl Scout treat of roasted marshmallows, Hershey bars, and graham crackers) as a celebration of letting go of the old and making a new beginning as a team.

 After a great deal of hostility and a bitter two-month labor union strike, key managers, union representatives, and Air Force personnel came together at Arnold Air Force Base to discuss the strike's long-term effects on morale, trust and teamwork. David Garner, chief steward for the machinist's union and secretary for the

AEMTC contract negotiations, said, "All participants came together on a first name basis, for risk-free, hierarchy-free critical planning sessions where we pledged to never allow relationships to deteriorate like that again." Because they kept referring to "Burying the hatchet," they decided to create a ceremony. A casket was built with 49 pre-drilled holes and participants placed a hatchet inside. Then each one drove in a nail to close it, and they buried it on Air Force property. It is still there with its own headstone as a reminder of what happened!

TIPS FOR IMPLEMENTATION:

Whenever I do focus groups in an organization, I ask them what they really love about working there and then what are the barriers to that being the very best place in the world to work. This allows them the opportunity to get negative feelings out in the open, and it provides excellent feedback to the organization. I then focus on their ideas for creative SOLUTIONS for each of the barriers as a way of "moving on" and changing negative energy into positive action.

Another concrete way to allow people to let go of barriers in a kinesthetic way is to write them on a piece of paper and then either crumple that paper up and throw it in the waste basket or even make a paper airplane and "fly the barriers away." When employees have an opportunity to set aside or to let go of the barriers they perceive as hindering their doing their best work, it then allows them to be able to take *individual responsibility* to change what is within their control and to let go of the "victim" mentality. The more creatively you make this happen, the more memorable and powerful it is to participants.

Create an Atmosphere of Encouragement

THE IDEA:

If the physical atmosphere in an organization is inviting and encouraging, people will feel better about coming to work and thus, will be more productive.

"I see you finally moved in Johnson. I like what you've done with your office."

THE IDEA IN ACTION:

When I visited the Cedar Falls Center of APAC TeleServices, I was immediately impacted by the bright colors and positive, uplifting atmosphere. Right inside the door was a display of all the prizes the associates could win for exceeding their goals, a wonderful visual encouragement. Next, on a side wall was a huge graph in the shape of a pizza that read "PIZZA—PIZZA: LET'S BEAT IOWA CITY!" This was a constant reminder of a fun internal contest they had created. The losing center had to buy the other center pizza.

Throughout the center there were large signs and banners posted in bright colors:

There is no "I" in team

Every time you make another call, no matter how many times you've heard the script, this is **THEIR FIRST TIME!**

Speak positively about each other and the organization you serve.

In helping others, you help yourself!

In every cubicle the APAC mission statement was prominently displayed. Another wall had a bright chart translating what achieving 100 percent, 110 percent, 120 percent and 130 percent of their goals would mean to each employee in extra pay per hour, *really* showing in a concrete way "what is in it for them!"

As I walked around, the atmosphere permeated all the work that was going on, and I heard employees who really felt good about their jobs and the difference they were making.

 The founder of a pediatric dental office in Oakland, California, has created a very special atmosphere for his patients and employees. He feels people should learn about healing in a fun and happy place. All the pictures are at the children's eye level, including the bulletin board with pictures of the other dentists and employees as children themselves. Bright colors, "theme" rooms, stuffed animals hanging from the ceilings, and a "yellow brick road" to help the children find their way all add to the happy atmosphere. The doctor tells this story as one of the best affirmations he has ever had about the vision he has created:

He had been noticing an older man eating his lunch in the waiting room for several days. Finally, he asked him one day, "Do your grandchildren come here to get their teeth fixed?" He answered, "No." "Are you waiting for someone?" "No," he answered. When the doctor finally asked in a kindly way why he was there, the man replied, "I used to be the postman for your office, and it always brightened my day to come here. Now I'm retired, and I just like to come here to eat my lunch and watch."

TIPS FOR IMPLEMENTATION:

Let employees get involved in brightening up the atmosphere. Tom Peters admonishes us to "fight boredom and sterility." Have a "poster party" and ask employees to bring in their favorite sayings or quotations. Provide flip chart pads, colored markers, and snacks. You will be amazed at the talent you didn't even know existed! Then laminate these and post them all over the building to create a positive, motivating environment.

Promote a Philosophy That the Workplace Should Be Fun

THE IDEA:

If people enjoy coming to work, they will be happier and, as a result, more productive. Plan activities that everyone will enjoy and will look forward to. Favorite activities will often develop into organizational traditions.

THE IDEA IN ACTION:

Miriam Beam and Angie Skaggs, the Managers of Training and Service at Foster & Gallagher in Peoria, Illinois, say: "One of the reasons we enjoy being part of the Customer Sales and Services group is the philosophy that our jobs should be a fun place to come every day. This makes it easier to create a fun atmosphere. We have a party of some sort every month and small 'perks' at other times. The following are some of the activities that happen to ease stress and spark enthusiasm":

> St. Patrick's Day Party—The employees dressed in green, and we provided green punch and shamrock cookies. We had contests centered around Irish trivia, "Mr. Potatohead" decorating with a real potato, Irish food judging by anyone who wanted to enter, and an area decorating contest for each group. We always have all of the activities for the day, evening, and weekend shifts.

"TAKE A NUMBER."

Spring Break—We had a Spring Break party where everyone had a box lid full of sand, and they created a sand scene. The scenes went from sand volleyball to "Baywatch." We gave away beach balls and served non-alcoholic drinks with umbrellas in them. Beach attire was the dress for the party (within reason, of course!).

Our busy season for hiring for the holidays begins in September. We had a baby picture contest for all the current employees with the slogan "We all started somewhere." There were quizzes they could do at their desks on actors and actresses and their real name matchup and other activities related to babies. We gave away prizes like big choco-late pacifiers from one of our gift catalogs.

On Halloween we have a costume judging contest, and this year we are having a haunted house for all to experience. There is a pumpkin carving contest along with a pumpkin pie contest. We have people from the other divisions act as judges for the various contests.

Around the Christmas holidays we have the "Tree of Lights" raf-fle for the Salvation Army. We solicit prizes from the local businesses and sell raffle tickets to the employees. The number of prizes we receive determines how many prizes can be awarded. We also have an ornament exchange to help decorate the Christmas tree. At the end of the season, those that brought an ornament can pick another ornament to take home.

During National Customer Service Week, we had several activi-ties. One of them was an alphabet soup potluck. Each team randomly draws a few letters of the alphabet and then on the day of the potluck, the team brings food which begins with those letters. We get some crazy foods!

A dart board contest is another of many favorites. After the rep reaches a sales goal, they get three darts to throw at a bal-loon board. Each balloon contains a slip of paper listing the prize they won. Prizes include extended breaks, soda, candy, etc.

We also have crazy fun days which include crazy hat day, bad hair day, Easter bonnet day, theme days, and more.

Miriam and Angie say, "We have the reps from time to time cre-ate their own contests which have proven to be successful since it was their idea. It is a fun environment, and you never know what will be next!"

TIPS FOR IMPLEMENTATION:

Use all the creativity of your staff to come up with creative, fun ideas just as Miriam and Angie did. Several of the reasons for their successes, I think, are: 1) They provide the same activities for ALL the shifts. Sometimes organizations forget about the evening shifts and just do activities in the daytime, so part of the staff is left out of the spirit. 2) They occasionally use prizes and treats FROM THEIR OWN CUSTOMER CATALOGS. When reps are familiar with a product, they are much more likely to feel good about it and sell it. 3) They use people from other parts of the company to judge the contests, so they spread the spirit throughout the company as well as giving other divisions ideas. 4) They are doing things as a group for others (Salvation Army), so the whole focus is not just internal. 5) They are recognizing the Supervisors, which is KEY in having a spirited staff. 6) They encourage staff to come up with their own ideas, getting their creative juices going and involving them beyond "just doing their jobs." Don't forget to celebrate diverse holidays and occasions as well.

Here are a few other great ideas from companies with whom I've worked:

> January—Super Bowl Party the Friday before the Super Bowl. Employees dress casually in the colors of their favorite team. At lunch breaks show NFL Blooper videos and snack on popcorn, peanuts, and pretzels.

> April—Baseball is back! On opening day, employees dress in the colors of their favorite (or local) team. At lunch serve hot-dogs and chips.

> September—Back to school! Encourage employees to dress as they did in high school. Bring in their high school pictures and vote on the most and least changed. Another option is to make Fridays in September casual days and employees bring in school supplies. Then these are donated to needy children.

Create "Time Out" Places

THE IDEA:

Create places in your work environment (besides the bathrooms) where people can go to get away for a few moments, almost like the "time out" corners or chairs most of us remember from our grade school days.

THE IDEA IN ACTION:

A well-traveled colleague recently told me that in downtown Tokyo, Japan, "nap" hotels are becoming popular. You can rent a lounge chair for $4 an hour and a small tent for $7 an hour in a "quiet room." Think about creating a place in your building where someone might go for a 10-minute vacation or even a cathartic pillow-beating exercise like the old encounter group days! I heard of one company that had a small room with a dart board. Employees could post anyone's picture with whom they were disgruntled and "release" their negative energy by filling it full of darts! Another company's employees installed a "Porta Potty" at the end of a long, quiet hall as a private, get-away-from-it-all "thinking place!"

> I want people to get what's in their heads into our shareholder's pocketbooks and have a good time doing it.
>
> LOU NOTO, PRESIDENT AND CEO
> *Mobil Oil Company*

TIPS FOR IMPLEMENTATION:

Be creative and a bit silly as you approach this idea! Employees will love the craziness and will transfer their negative energy to positive energy in laughing and talking about the "time out" place whether or not they ever use it. Be sure, however, that you create some sort of an "in use" or "vacant" sign so that no one's privacy is compromised.

Create an Atmosphere of Caring Competition

THE IDEA:

Competition in the workplace can be either an assassinator or a regenerator of spirit. In many workplaces where I've spoken, I find such a strong competitive drive that employees are pitted one against another, and the result is a divided workforce, each out to get the best for himself/herself. The key is to create an atmosphere of competitive caring where the competition is friendly and fun, and the important end result is not on individuals but on how the whole team performs.

THE IDEA IN ACTION:

I recently had the delightful experience of conducting several focus groups in the Oskaloosa, Iowa, center of APAC Corporation, a tele-services company. I discovered there the epitome of an atmosphere of caring competition. One of the Telephone Service Reps in the group told me, "Some honest caring goes on here." When I asked them what they loved about working at APAC, one of the reps said, "We get to travel all over the world, yet we never have to leave home." What an amazingly positive, creative attitude she expressed!

The center manager, Shane Zickefoose, exemplifies what every manager should strive for. His office is a large table right out in the middle of the center, not back in a room with a door. He makes it a point to regularly spend time on the phones and to be out on the floor, coaching and encouraging his employees. From my time there, I could see that he was not only their manager but also their friend.

He encourages his supervisors to create an atmosphere of friendly competition. As one TSR put it, "We cheer for EVERY-BODY!" They play games such as Hangman and Wheel of Fortune where a rep gets a letter for each sale. Another game they use is Dominoes. Each time a rep gets a sale, he/she gets to reach in a bag and pick a domino. At the end of the game, the person with the most/least dots wins. The prize may be money, APAC clothing, or even getting to leave early.

What amazed me even more was that this center was in an old building that had a problem with fleas (they are planning to move in just a few months), and the employees STILL had a wonderfully positive team spirit and really loved their jobs!

TIPS FOR IMPLEMENTATION:

Competition in the workplace can either be motivating or de-motivating for employees. The key is to make it fun, not cutthroat, and to ensure that everyone has a chance to win. Most of all, emphasize the team effort above individual effort so that every employee can feel pride in his or her organization.

Part Two:

THE JOY OF PLEASANT SURPRISES AT WORK

"Call 911 and put out a memo, No more surprise parties."

Spontaneous Treats

THE IDEA:

Spontaneous treats for employees really add a special joy to the atmosphere, one of saying "thanks," especially when tough situations occur.

THE IDEA IN ACTION:

 When the air-conditioning broke down on one of the hottest days of the year, the office manager ran out to the local grocery store and bought popsicles for every employee. They then had a "stripping" ceremony where everyone took off their ties and pantyhose! The manager turned a horrible day into one that will long be remembered.

 Another organization has a "surprise treat" day once a month. On that day the managers do things like renting a popcorn machine or serving everyone coffee and donuts at their desks or "borrowing" an ice cream cart and delivering ice cream bars throughout the building. It is a special way of saying "Thanks for doing such good work."

 Ashley Glanz, the Director of the ABC Nursery and Day Camp in Chicago, Illinois, was anticipating a hard day because two of her teachers were going to be out sick. On her way to work she stopped at the store and bought Nestle's Crunch bars. When she arrived at work, she placed a Crunch bar on each teacher's desk with a note, "Thanks for helping out in the *Crunch*!"

TIPS FOR IMPLEMENTATION:

It is important to do things that will fit your culture, but don't be afraid to have a little fun. We all need to "lighten up" now and then. All the research shows that spontaneous or surprise rewards get much more attention and response than things that are planned, so put this book down now and surprise someone!

Adding Enhancements

THE IDEA:

Whenever employees are encouraged to add enhancements to their customers' experiences, it makes their job much more fun and regenerates the spirit in their workplace, wherever that may be.

THE IDEA IN ACTION:

Fred Evenson from the State of Michigan tells a story about being stopped by a patrolman as he and his family were traveling on vacation in Montana:

> I was stopped for exceeding the speed limit as we traveled through Montana. This was at the time when the national speed limit was 55 MPH. The state of Montana was pushing for a 70 MPH speed limit. The Montana patrolman clocked me at 10 MPH over the speed limit. He explained to me that he was going to give me a "daytime" ticket which would be cheaper than a "nighttime" ticket. The nighttime ticket cost $50 while the ticket he gave me was $5. Not only did he show flexibility and relieve my worries of an unexpected added expense on an already tight budget, but he also returned to our car with Montana Highway Patrol coloring books for each of my children! He definitely made what could have been for us a very negative situation into a positive, memorable one.

Jill Mallinder, the Manager of Documentation and Training Development at Rockwell International in Downers Grove, Illinois, told me about a situation last year when they realized that their customers had received an incorrect set of documentation for a software product. This was part of the letter Jill sent to them:

> Enclosed is the correct set of documentation. We have included instructions to help you know how to replace these documents in the binders you already have. We apologize for the inconvenience and have updated the configurator number so it won't happen again. We've also tucked into the box a packet of hot chocolate mix. Once you've spent the 15 minutes changing your books, treat yourself to a hot cup of cocoa!

Another manager, during a very stressful time for her employees put a package of tea bags and a small bottle of bubble bath on each employee's desk with a note to "do something nice for themselves" that night! I even heard of an employee who, when it was the middle of tax season in her accounting firm, put a package of LIFESAVERS™ on each of her co-workers' desks with a note saying, "Hang in there—only 21 more days to go!"

Cheryl Birdsley of the Michigan Department of State shares how she *literally* made her customers and employees smile:

> While managing the downtown Lansing office several years ago, many customers would come in and complain about their pictures on their driver's license. I thought about props that professional photographers use, so I bought a yellow squeaky rubber ducky and "Groucho Marx" glasses with a mustache and bushy eyebrows. When I took the customer's picture, instead of asking if they'd like to smile, I'd put on the glasses and come up over the camera with the "Groucho Marx" surprise. The customer would laugh and Voila! I'd get a smile, and the customer would leave laughing. In the process clerks would also crack up at the customer's response, and the tension in the packed office would dissipate.

A consultant working with Saint Francis Medical Center in Peoria, Illinois, would occasionally throughout his day there hear lullaby music. When on a tour of the facility, he inquired about the music. He was told that every time a new baby is born, they play a portion of Brahm's lullaby! They do this because hospitals can so often be associated with sickness and death that they wanted to share the joy that is also present in the celebration of new life. If a birth occurs at night, they wait until the following morning to play the lullaby.

TIPS FOR IMPLEMENTATION:

Whenever possible, do something to enhance the customer's experience, remembering both internal and external customers. It might be a special "giveaway," some additional information or education, or even advice about something other than the business at hand.

The creativity and spontaneity involved can add excitement and fun to an otherwise mundane job.

Joyful Surprises

THE IDEA:

Think of special ways you can surprise others and add joy to their sometimes extremely difficult days.

THE IDEA IN ACTION:

> Give a compliment to someone you don't know in your company or building.
>
> Pick up someone's mail and deliver it to them.
>
> Give a small anonymous gift to a co-worker who is down.
>
> Drop off a small plant to another department that supports you.
>
> Call someone in the company just to say, "I appreciate you."
>
> Surprise a co-worker with a newspaper or magazine he/she would enjoy.
>
> Bring ice cream back after your lunch hour to the custodial staff (or mailroom or shipping).

Two machinists, Claude Jean and Mike Newman, who work in the small parts sub-factory at Menasco Aerospace in Oakville, Ontario, Canada, are hard workers with a sense of humor.

Claude and Mike's work station is at a busy crossroad of an aisleway in the plant. There are wood partitions that divide the aisle from their work station. Every day Claude and Mike post interesting newspaper articles, results of the Menasco hockey team, and other items of great interest on the outside of the partition, enticing personnel to stop and read the posted material. Most of the people who stop to read the things on the board grab the top or the side of the partition as they read. As they do so, they quietly receive a free "manicure" with brightly colored nail polish by either Claude or Mike on the other side. The "victims" all of a sudden at a meeting, in the cafeteria, or even when they get home, discover their polished nails and have no idea how this happened. It has given many Menasco employees a good chuckle!

TIPS FOR IMPLEMENTATION:

Try to think of people in your workplace who truly need a lift—and then surprise them. You might even think of something as fun as Claude and Mike!

Decorate for the Holidays in Places Where It Surprises People

THE IDEA:

Find places in your workplace where holiday decorations will surprise and delight your co-workers and customers. You might even consider decorating the restrooms!

THE IDEA IN ACTION:

 At the airport in Cedar Rapids, Iowa, Karen Ealy, a Supervisor, has made it her special gift to both employees and customers to decorate the tops of the security detector machines for each holiday. It changes a rather frightening experience for new travelers and a somewhat aggravating routine experience for seasoned travelers to one of delight and appreciation, and it also makes the wait in line much more palatable. She says that busy executives even thank her for reminding them of the holidays like Valentine's Day and Mother's Day that they are likely to forget!

 I recently received this letter from employees of the Michigan Department of State:

All of us wanted to express the enthusiasm and excitement that we all felt after attending your seminar! In keeping with the spirit of making our job more exciting (for both us and our customers!), we have pledged our devotion to making our office a fun, more enjoyable place to work. It's nearly Halloween again, and thanks to the help of our resident decorating specialist, we have transformed our office into a creative Halloween haven!

As customers come into our office, they now walk through gigantic balloon arches that loom above the front doors. A lifesize grim reaper with blinking eyes decorates one part of the office, and Count Dracula waits in another area. Bats hover around the ceiling, close to a group of fearsome spiders—and we're not sure how he got in, but a rather large spider created a monstrous web that hangs over our customers' heads!

We have a pumpkin patch in one area made out of balloons—each pumpkin has the name of an employee on it. There is a balloon centerpiece on each computer, a balloon witch on the wall, and several ghosts haunting the ceiling as well. And our manager's office has been renamed "Dracula's Den." Our District Manager is now called the "Dungeon Master" and quite surprisingly, we don't have as many children misbehaving as we did before!

Many of these changes have come about thanks to the work you put into helping us and the way you have changed our attitudes about customer service. We really can make a difference (and we are!!!!)

TIPS FOR IMPLEMENTATION:

Try to include decorations for holidays from all cultures and religions since many travelers are far away from home and would truly appreciate this gesture of caring. Sharing other's holiday traditions also celebrates diversity and teaches a bit about another culture.

Help People Through the "Tough" Days

THE IDEA:

Concern for your employees during particularly stressful times will not only improve morale by giving them a feeling of being cared for, but it will also take their minds off the stress.

THE IDEA IN ACTION:

At Duke Power Company in Charlotte, North Carolina, they have many stressful days in their call center, which is open 24 hours a day, seven days a week, and handles an average of six million calls a year. Michael Landrum, the manager of Customer Service Consulting, says that they consider employees as important as the customers, and they treat them that way. Especially during stressful times, they support and affirm their employees. When the center was installing a new voice response unit, they removed the old one and then held a funeral for it, complete with a viewing and a coffin!

The Tuesday following a holiday Monday is particularly difficult for employees because of the huge number of calls they get. Landrum says, "Even if our measurements say that we're not as good as usual, we know how hard the specialists are working just to keep pace, so we hand out ice cream to say thanks for handling so many calls and taking so much heat from customers. We're amazed at the difference it makes. After handing out the ice cream, we'll check the service level, and it has greatly improved, even with the extra challenges of the day."

Ken Hakala, an assistant branch manager, for the Michigan Department of State shares how he uses his own special creativity to brighten up the hard days:

> One 90-degree day in May, the employees of the office were in irritable moods. The customers were uncomfortable in the hot building, and I had to think of something to change the atmosphere of the office. I began to whistle Christmas tunes! At first the employees thought that I had lost my marbles, but then laughter started to permeate the office and a negative situation quickly became a positive one!

The February 2, 1994, edition of the *Chicago Tribune* contained an article titled "Stand-up guy: Jerry Ingram brings comic relief to the fearful business of surgery." Jerry is an orderly at the Russo Surgical Pavilion at Loyola University Medical Center in Maywood, Illinois, and he brings a special gift of humor and caring to his job. When most orderlies in most hospitals arrive with the cart to take a patient to surgery, it's like the coming of the Grim Reaper, and patients are apprehensive and fearful and families are nervous wrecks. But Ingram, a 6 foot 4 inch 31 year old man, has made it his business "to try to make my little difference the best way I can. Some of the stuff I say, I don't know why they laugh. But they do." He walks in smiling his big grin and reads the chart to find out something about them that might provide an opener, and then he keeps them laughing all the way to surgery.

> When people work in a place that cares about them, they contribute a lot more than duty.
>
> **DENNIS HAYES, CEO**
> *Hayes Microcomputer Products, Inc.*

At the entrance to the operating room, he instructs the family to line up to kiss the patient, and then he announces, "Save the best for last!" and kisses the patient on the cheek. "Remember," he adds, "we don't believe in luck. We believe in prayers, and she has mine."

His boss, Esther Isaac, says that Ingram's encouraging banter with patients is "very instrumental in helping break the tension . . . It's not minimizing the gravity of the situation. It's welcome. His intent is what's appreciated. He's genuine. He likes people. He likes his job." And one of the nurses says, "Patients just love Jerry," and he is the one they remember after they leave. Jerry Ingram certainly is regenerating the spirits of all in his place of work![1]

> A great man is one who has not lost his child's heart.
>
> **MENCIUS**

TIPS FOR IMPLEMENTATION:

You can become a stress reliever whether you're a manager or an employee of an organization. Just get your creative juices going and have some fun!

Lighten Up on Dress Codes

THE IDEA:

"Working Life," a column in *Training & Development* magazine, shared a nationwide study of 750 employees conducted by Campbell

Research and Levi Strauss in its February 1995 issue. 46 percent of respondents say that dress would be a factor in accepting job offers, all other things being equal. Ninety-six percent say they take advantage of their companies' casual dress days, and 65 percent of senior-level managers participate. Eighty-one percent of respondents feel that casual dress improves morale; 47 percent say it improves productivity.[2] If, however, you feel that it is essential for your organization to have a dress code, then have fun with it rather than make it a punishment.

THE IDEA IN ACTION:

 A company I consulted had a stiff dress code, and employees were unhappy about it. One of the Telephone Service Representatives suggested the following. Instead of sending people home to change when they are dressed inappropriately, go to some resale shops and buy lots of gross-looking polyester clothes. Then keep them in a box or closet and when someone doesn't adhere to the dress code, they have to wear something from "the polyester box" for the rest of the day. This quickly solved the problem!

 Rosenbluth Travel uses dress to have fun in their place of work. Some days they dress like their accounts or clients, wearing clothing that has that company's logo. Sometimes people wear costumes that reflect their favorite destination in a contest to get there.[3]

 A bank I work with has a "Casual Day" every Friday during the summer months. Each year they purchase knit golf shirts of a different color with the bank logo on them, and all employees wear these shirts on Fridays. According to both floor traffic and customer feedback, the customers especially love banking on this day!

TIPS FOR IMPLEMENTATION:

Evaluate the amount of negative energy that is spent both on enforcing and complaining about the dress code in your organization. Also consider the hardship it causes for employees on minimum wage, especially if they become pregnant or change sizes.

Even requiring nylons for the women can cause an overwhelming expense for some workers. Does employee dress truly impact the productivity or image of your organization or is this the way "it's always been"? If you do decide that a dress code is necessary, be as specific as you can in terms of what is acceptable and unacceptable attire, i.e., Is chambray considered the same as denim? Are knee high nylons acceptable? I suggest photographs of various degrees of unacceptability, but make these funny so that workers can still maintain some self-respect.

Notes

1. Lauerman, Connie. 1994. "Stand-up guy." *Chicago Tribune*, Section 5, Wednesday, 2 February, pp. 1, 5.

2. Allerton, Haidee. 1995. "Working Life: Tired of Being PC." *Training & Development*, February, pp. 71–72.

3. Rosenbluth, Hal & McFerrin, Diane. 1992. *The Customer Comes Second*, New York, NY: William Morrow and Company, Inc.

Personal Action Ideas

Write your ideas here!

"Thanks men. I finally got up on one ski."

CHAPTER

V

A = APPRECIATION FOR ALL

Just as the accumulation of small improvements can make a dramatic, lasting change in the organization's products or services, the repeated, numerous small occasions of taking note of the contributions of individuals and teams of individuals can create a different company.

PATRICK TOWNSEND AND JOAN GEBHARDT
"The Quality Process: Little Things Mean a Lot"
Review of Business, Winter 1990/1991

"Daily Affirmations: Seeing the Small Wonders All Around You"

Mark Twain said, "I can go two months on one good compliment!" The most valuable assets in any organization are the people who work there. Quality people produce quality products and services. If you're able to increase the value of your co-workers, you create a more valuable company.

One of the most important ways to increase the value of those with whom you work is to appreciate them. In fact, it is the number two thing people want from their jobs, even before money and promotions. A study by Robert Half International, a Menlo Park, California, staffing services firm, found that 34 percent of 150 executives recently surveyed said limited recognition and praise was the most common reason employees leave companies.[1]

William James, the great American psychologist said, "The deepest principle in human nature is the craving to be appreciated." The Bible says, "Encourage each other and build each other up." In his book *The Greatest Management Principle in the World* Michael LeBoeuf tells us that what every employee really wants is to be recognized and rewarded. The greatest management principle in the world is "The things that get rewarded get done." Appreciation is the most important kind of reward one can get.

According to *Stew's News*, the company newsletter for Stew Leonard's Connecticut-based grocery stores, there are three characteristics of effective appreciation:

- It is genuine, from the heart.
- It is clear and specific.
- It is regular—not just on special occasions.

Bob Nelson, the author of 1001 *Ways to Reward Employees* (Workman, 1994), says this about appreciation:

> Everyone likes to be appreciated. How many managers, however, consider "appreciating others" to be a major function of their job today? It should be. At a time in which employees are being asked to do more than ever before, the resources and support for helping them is at an all time low. Budgets are tight; salaries are frozen. Managers tend to be too busy and too removed from their employees to notice when they have done exceptional work—and to thank them for it. Technology has replaced personal interaction with one's manager with constant interfacing with one's terminal. And all this is happening at a time in which employees are looking to have greater meaning in their lives—and especially in their jobs.
>
> The irony of the situation is that what motivates people the most takes so relatively little to do—just a little time and thoughtfulness

for starters. In a recent research study of 1500 employees conducted by Dr. Gerald Graham, personal congratulations by managers of employees who do a good job was ranked first from 67 potential incentives he evaluated. Second was a personal note for good performance written by the manager. Make the extra effort to appreciate your employees, and they'll reciprocate in a thousand ways.

As Ken Blanchard said in *The One Minute Manager*, "Make a habit of catching people doing something right!" Not only will it make them feel good, but it will change the spirit in your place of work when you begin to truly appreciate others. You don't have to be a manager to thank someone for a job well done!

"Pass It On" Cards

THE IDEA:

Everyone likes to receive a surprise, especially if it is one that involves appreciation. And it is even more fun if the surprise can be a part of an ongoing process.

THE IDEA IN ACTION:

One of my personal signatures is that whenever I speak to a group, I give each person in the group a "PASS IT ON"™ card (published by Argus Communications, Allen, TX) which has a butterfly on it and says on the front, *"Some people make the world more special just by being in it."* On the back it reads "PASS IT ON"™. I ask them to give this card in the next 48 hours to someone who has done some little thing to make a difference in their lives. These cards are available from Argus Communications; however, several organizations with whom I've worked have created their own.

TIPS FOR IMPLEMENTATION:

The preprinted cards come with a variety of sayings on them. These are a few of my favorites:

The difference between ordinary and extraordinary is that little "extra"!

Do you mind if I appreciate you?

What you are is God's gift to you; what you become is your gift to God.

Choose one that feels good to you and that will not offend the person to whom you give it, or even have a variety of cards for different people. These are also easy to create on the computer and can be put in lunches, desk drawers, pockets, in bills and notes, or stuck under office doors as a special surprise.

The difference between ordinary and **extra**ordinary is that little **EXTRA.**

The Silver Dollar CARE Award

THE IDEA:

Every organization needs to foster more daily appreciation. The challenge is to come up with creative ways to reward and appreciate employees on a continuous basis and to make these rewards fair (available to every employee), fun (capture their attention and make then WANT to get the reward), and of value (reinforce behaviors and values that are important to the organization).

THE IDEA IN ACTION:

The Clarion Hotel in Virginia Beach, VA, a part of Manor Care Hotels, gives every employee a "CARE Credo Card" as a reminder to associates of their very important role in caring for customers. These cards are laminated, and each employee is asked to carry the card at all times when they are working.

> The happiness of life is made up of minute fractions — the little soon forgotten charities of a kiss or smile, a kind look, a heartfelt compliment, and the countless infinitesimals of pleasurable and genial feeling.
>
> SAMUEL TAYLOR COLERIDGE

Every week, the General Manager picks a "mystery manager" and gives that person five silver dollars. During the week, as this manager interacts with the employees, he asks them three questions:

1. Do you have your CARE card with you?

2. Can you recite one letter and what it means?

3. What did you do today either for a customer or to assist another person with a customer that represents that letter?

If the person can answer all three questions positively, he or she gets the silver dollar and their name is recorded. Each month at the general pep rally a drawing of the 20 winners is held, and the winner receives a day off with pay. John Giattino, the general manager, feels this means of positive recognition not only reinforces employee empowerment but it also reinforces the company's values in a creative and fun way.

> If you show people you don't care, they'll return the favor. Show them you care about them, they'll reciprocate.
>
> LEE G. BOLMAN AND TERRENCE E. DEAL
> Leading with Soul: An Uncommon Journey of Spirit

TIPS FOR IMPLEMENTATION:

Remember that no matter how good a recognition program is, it will get old over time. Involve your employees in helping create new ways to reward and recognize those who are living by company values. It will enhance their creative spirits as well as gain their commitment by encouraging them to be a part of the process.

Creative and Personal Appreciations

THE IDEA:

How do you appreciate others around you? Doing this creatively will help you stand out in a really positive way. Get your creative juices going to determine some unusual, attention-getting, delightful ways you can thank others in your life. Consider a fishbowl of cartoons, jokes or positive thoughts, special post-it notes to leave, affirming stickers, handwritten notes of any kind, bringing a picnic lunch to share with someone, and of course, any kind of treats.

THE IDEA IN ACTION:

A friend recently sent a business colleague and internal customer the following huge 3-D "treat" card:

> *You are* **CERTStainly** *a* **LIFESAVER** *and worth* $100,000 *to us! Sometimes life is a* **ROCKY ROAD** *but* **BAR NONE** *you are always* **MOUNDS** *of* **JOY,** *laughs, and* **SNICKERS!** *You are a* **BOUNTY** *of fun, very* **CAREFREE,** *and* **EXTRA** *special.* **SKOR** *big and count down to* **PAYDAY.** *Best wishes, hugs, and* **KISSES!**

Rita Emmett, the Coordinator of Educational Programs at Leyden Family Service and Mental Health Center in Franklin Park, Illinois, brought in flowers for everyone in the office on her five-year anniversary of quitting smoking. They loved it so much that now she watches for carnations on sale in the grocery stores. When they are, she declares a "Flower Day" and surprises each employee with one as a special appreciation for their help and support.

Jim Munroe, Operations Coordinator of the Program for Employee Participation at Santee Cooper, the public power company owned by the people of South Carolina, sends poems by E-mail to appreciate his co-workers and especially to wish them a Happy Birthday. He has received so much affirmation for doing this that he is now known as "The Workplace Poet"!

This one was sent to a Stores Specialist who does warehouse work:

> You stock the shelves and that's not all,
> Shipping, receiving and telephone calls,
> Forms for this and forms for that,
> You even take care of old stray cats!
> So jump on that forklift and drive away,
> Have some cake and ice cream and a Happy Birthday!

To an Investment Recovery Agent who does reclamation and recycling:

> You take old equipment, sometimes it's our trash,
> You recycle the stuff and make lots of cash.
> We send in our bids for the cars, boats, and chairs,
> For office equipment and I'm looking for hair!
> We really appreciate all the recycling you do,
> I ask but one question—Can you recycle us, too?

To their Payroll Administrator:

> You deal with the payroll all the day long
> And hear all kinds of complaints if something is wrong.
> In this day and time we need to daily give thanks
> For at least we have something to take to our banks.
> It must be lots of fun handling all of that dough
> Every two weeks you play Santa and make our face glow.
> Thanks for doing a great job, we know you won't fail.
> But please just don't tell me, "Your check's in the mail!"

He then ends each note with an inspirational quotation.
I feel very honored that Jim wrote this poem just for me:

The sign said "ESCAPE YOUR COCOON AND FLY FREE."
That certainly was not the seminar for me!
But COMMUNICATION is a tool I use every day
And I might learn something CREATIVE, somehow, some way.
Barbara Glanz was her name, the consultant who C.A.R.E.s.
She says, "MAKE A DIFFERENCE," but you better beware.
Cause she speaks to your head and also your heart,
Your fire is rekindled and a journey will start.
Soon "SPIRIT IN THE WORKPLACE" will be commonplace
And the load will be lighter with a smile on your face.
Your CUSTOMERS will notice this super new look
And remain LOYAL if you practice the things in her books.
"ENTHUSIASM IS CONTAGIOUS," just catch it and see,
It will make a BIG difference in your company.

Thanks, Jim!

 Whenever I speak to a group on "C.A.R.E. Packages for the Work-place," I give each person in the audience a small 1" by 2" brown cardboard box with the letters "C.A.R.E." stamped on it as a remembrance of the ideas I've shared with them. I gave one of these boxes to Richard Narramore, my editor for this book, when I first began to write. He recently shared with me that he had "passed it on" to Ennise, another person in his office, with three quarters in it and a note of appreciation suggesting that she buy herself a soda on him. He then asked her to pass the C.A.R.E. box on to someone else filled with "something creative" from her own special spirit.

No matter where you are, you can find or make a small box of some sort, write the letters C.A.R.E. on it, and fill it with a surprise to appreciate someone in your place of work. Then ask them to pass it on, adding their own special spirit.

TIPS FOR IMPLEMENTATION:

It is important to honor your own comfort level in giving appreciation. Choose what feels "right" for you, but always keep in mind the element of surprise!

Create a "Just Because . . ." Committee

THE IDEA:

Create a volunteer committee from across departments, perhaps spearheaded by someone in HR, to plan special events to appreciate your employees.

THE IDEA IN ACTION:

Diane Hawkins of Rockwell International in Downers Grove, Illinois, chairs this committee in her workplace. They plan special events for the employees about every other month. Here are some of the things they have done:

 All employees were invited during the lunch hour to come for hot dogs, hamburgers, and brats in the parking lot. Grills were set up, and people could even bring their small children.

 For "Beat the Winter Blues," the committee sponsored a Yahtzee competition in the lunchroom with prizes.

 On Valentine's Day they put a chocolate heart on each employee's desk with a card that said, "Just because . . ."

 Also at Christmas they send a Rockwell calendar and candy to the home of each employee.

 One month they had a Mexican theme at lunch with pinatas and a "make your own taco" party.

TIPS FOR IMPLEMENTATION:

Let employees plan these events, and try to get as many departments as possible on the committee to ensure buy-in. Give them a budget for the year, and then let their creativity blossom! Not only will they learn lots about event planning, but you will also have a much happier and therefore more productive workplace.

Appreciate Your Employees as *Individuals*

THE IDEA:

Sometimes in showing our appreciation, we give others a generic reward or even what WE think they would like. To truly recognize someone in a special, caring way, concentrate on that person as a unique individual.

THE IDEA IN ACTION:

 At Blanchard Training and Development in San Diego, California, Ken Blanchard, whose new title is "Chief Spiritual Officer," as a special surprise gave each of the 125 employees $50 with the following instructions:

"You each have one hour and 15 minutes to go out and do something special *just for yourself*. At the end of that time, come back and each of you tell us your story."

This creative surprise to appreciate their employees not only added wonderful fun and spirit for that day, but more importantly contributed to company legend by creating lots of stories.

Another way the Blanchards showed special appreciation for their employees was taking the entire company with the exception of a skeleton crew who volunteered to man the phones to the International Conference of the American Society for Training and Development. This was not only a fun trip for them, but they also got to learn more about the training industry of which Blanchard T&D is a part, and they were able to attend sessions that contributed to their own professional growth and development. The eight people who stayed behind to man the office were treated to a special appreciation luncheon.

At Enterprise Systems in Wheeling, Illinois, $1500 in gift certificates are available for employees to give to one another for special appreciation. The presenter writes a sentence or two about why the award was given, and they decide the amount and the way they want to present the certificate. Each employee at the beginning of the year fills out a form listing things they would like to receive for recognition such as theater or sports tickets, dinner at a certain restaurant, a beauty treatment, etc. That way the presenter knows exactly what would please that particular employee and can give them a certificate for a uniquely special thank you. Also, employees have come up with some really creative ways to present the certificates, so many spirits are regenerated!

TIPS FOR IMPLEMENTATION:

Rewards and recognition, to be truly meaningful, should be given to the individual in a way that says, "YOU are special." Keep an "R and R" file with a list of each employee's or co-worker's interests and hobbies. Then USE this when planning a thank you just for them!

Affirm YOURSELF!

THE IDEA:

There are many times when we find our own emotional bank accounts are empty. These are the times when we need to do something special just for ourselves.

THE IDEA IN ACTION:

 Try taking a five minute vacation. This can be done physically by going outside and walking around the block or to another part of the building, or it can be a mental vacation. Close your eyes and vision a very special place that you have been or would like to go. Then do anything you'd like there, and the best part is that it won't cost you one penny! You'll be amazed at how refreshed you can feel in even five minutes.

> There are two things that people want more than sex and money— recognition and praise.
>
> **MARY KAY ASH, CEO**
> *Mary Kay Cosmetics*

 Jeff Davis, a trainer friend of mine, has created a poster with a large hand on it to give to the participants in his classes. It says, "Give yourself a hand!" He tells them to post it on the wall in their offices, and when they need some special affirmation, just back up to it and give themselves a pat on the back! [2]

> When we encourage others, we spur them on, we stimulate and affirm them. We appreciate what a person does, but we affirm who a person is.
>
> **CHARLES SWINDOLL**
> *Strengthening your Grip*

 Create an AIG ("Ain't I Great") folder for yourself. Fill it with cards, letters, notes, and awards that make you feel good. Then, when you're having a bad day, you can take it out and remember all the people who care about you. My daughter Erin has made collages in huge picture frames to hang in my office of cards, notes, and letters from clients, pictures of classes I've trained, and buttons, stickers, and little gifts they've given me. It helps me remember that I HAVE made a difference!

Barbara Johnson, the author of *Splashes of Joy in the Cesspools of Life*, suggests that we each keep a "JOY" box in which we put all kinds of little things that bring us joy. When my daughters went off to college, I gave each of them a special covered basket to be their "JOY" box, and during the year I sent them stories, cards, poems, letters, cartoons, and many little things to keep in it. Barbara Johnson's "JOY" boxes kept filling until she built an entire room on her house that then became her "JOY" room. I think of my office in that way. We all need more joy in our lives, so I hope you will find a place to collect those things that affirm YOU!

A delightful consultant friend of mine from Florida, says he sends *himself* flowers when he needs a lift. I love this idea! He says, "When you need love, ask for it OR give it to yourself."

TIPS FOR IMPLEMENTATION:

For many of us, it helps to have permission to affirm ourselves, so use this book as your special permission and start on your folder or box today! You might also want to give someone else a "JOY" box—you will be giving them permission, too.

Celebrate Small Successes or Near Misses

THE IDEA:

Remember it is important to celebrate small wins or even to recognize the efforts when a team comes close to a goal rather than just affirming when they reach it.

THE IDEA IN ACTION:

At Duke Power Company in Charlotte, North Carolina, teams in the call centers celebrate small successes with ice cream or watermelon parties because it is the small wins that lead to the large ones, and it also shows employees that you appreciate their efforts.

Michael Landrum, the Manager of Customer Service Consulting, says, "We make a point of celebrating 'near misses' where teams came close to reaching a goal but don't quite make it. These are 'near successes' to us and deserve recognition. Too many companies tend to ignore these, but business isn't like a ballgame where you have a winner and a loser. Let people feel successful even if they don't make the magical number that you set. If people improve from last year, they're successful, even if the improvement is only one or five percent."

TIPS FOR IMPLEMENTATION:

Think of fun, surprising, and creative ways to recognize the near misses and small wins. It will help morale immensely and will reinforce an emphasis on teamwork rather than always focusing on winning.

Daily Affirmations

THE IDEA:

Use different forms to show appreciation throughout the organization on a daily basis. Try something new at least once or twice a year.

THE IDEA IN ACTION:

W.O.W. (Within Our Walls)—This is a program at Lands' End for employees to recognize the positive things other employees do at any level. They fill out a form for the recognition, the person gets their picture posted with the recognition, and at the end of the month a drawing is held for a small gift. Bambi Grajek, the Phone Center Manager at Reedsburg, says, "The recognition could be for letting someone know that their lights are on or for always remembering to smile." Managers at Lands' End also recognize employees for perfect attendance.

To: _____ Date: _____

From: _____, your friend in Reedsburg.

I think you're great!

You really made a difference because _____

_____

_____

_____

LANDS' END
DIRECT MERCHANTS

 As I was waiting in the reception area at BI Performance Services, one of the people at the front desk was awarded the "Traveling Junk Trophy." This is an award that is given for doing something extraordinary for an internal customer. She was to add something "silly" to the trophy and then pass it on within the company. What a fun way to get rid of your junk AND celebrate someone's good deed!

TIPS FOR IMPLEMENTATION:

When you are initiating a program to encourage daily appreciation, be sure to have employees from all levels involved in the planning to ensure their buy-in and commitment. Then change it at least once a year. A suggestion—often at the end of the year companies recognize those employees who have received the most daily affirmations. Why not recognize as well those employees who have GIVEN the most daily affirmations? In many ways they are the true spirit builders!

The "Red Plate"

THE IDEA:

Whenever I work with a department or an organization over a period of time, I love to give them the "Red Plate." For many years the "Red Plate" has been our favorite family tradition. It is just that—a bright red plate with white hand-painted lettering along the edge that reads, "YOU ARE SPECIAL TODAY." It came with the following explanation:

> **Everyone in organizations should set as their goal to maintain or enhance the self esteem of the people with whom they interact.**
>
> **KEN BLANCHARD**
> *Blanchard Management Report*

The Red Plate is the perfect way to acknowledge a family member's special triumphs, to celebrate a birthday or praise a job well done, reward a goal achieved, or simply to say, "YOU ARE SPECIAL TODAY." When the Red Plate is used, any meal becomes a celebration honoring a special person, event, or deed. It is a visible reminder of love and esteem. The Red Plate— make it a tradition in your family, symbolizing the good and happy times. It will speak volumes of love when words just aren't enough.

THE IDEA IN ACTION:

The "Red Plate" is one of the best ways we have found to bring joy, affirmation, and encouragement to different members of our family and friends. Whenever we have a guest for dinner, he or she gets the "Red Plate." Whenever there is a special occasion—from birthdays, the first night home after being at camp or college, finishing a hard project, or getting a good grade on a test, that person gets the "Red Plate." (I have even heard of families who bring it with them to a restaurant when they are having a surprise party for someone!)

However, the most important use for our Red Plate, I think, has been for the hard times, those times when someone has worked and worked to get a part or make a team or win an election, and they have been disappointed. Someone in the family always makes sure they get the "Red Plate" that day as a symbol that they are still special, no matter what has happened.

Two years ago I gave the "Red Plate" as a gift to the publisher of my first two books, Irwin Professional Publishing in Burr Ridge, Illinois. I presented it to the Publisher at an all-company gathering where I was speaking. One of the most touching stories of its use was from a young man who is the receptionist in the building. He told us how surprised and delighted he was to be one of the first ones to get the "Red Plate." He said, "I thought only management would get it." He then decided that he would add his special touch, so when he passed the "Red Plate" on to someone who had made a difference for him, he put a Danish on it and thus began a new tradition in their organization!

> **We burn three times the energy when we think negatively than when we think positively.**
>
> **BOB PIKE, PRESIDENT**
> *Creative Training Techniques*

TIPS FOR IMPLEMENTATION:

> **It is one of the most beautiful compensations of this life that no man can sincerely try to help another without helping himself.**
>
> **RALPH WALDO EMERSON**

The "Red Plate" can be purchased at many Hallmark and gift stores or ordered from the address in the Resource section of the book on page 217. It is a fun and visible way to show appreciation in a company and also to create a new organizational tradition. Legends grow up around who got the "Red Plate" and why. Each person who receives it gets to keep it in his or her office for a certain period of time, and then they are asked to "pass it on." The "Red Plate" has been the bearer of many deposits in employees' emotional bank accounts!

"Wallow" in Your Successes

THE IDEA:

Find creative ways to share your pride in your organization and in one another.

THE IDEA IN ACTION:

 When I was Director of Quality in Training for Kaset International, Dave Erdman, the president of the company, started a tradition he called "Wallow Time." Whenever groups at Kaset got together to hold major planning and review meetings, Dave asked that they plan some "wallow" time. During "wallow time" the members of the group would share their pride at working with such a terrific group of people, tell each other the things they appreciated about one another, and share with the group the individual acts of support and kindness that others in the group had given them. Dave said, "We wallow in how good we are, how good we are to each other, and how much we really care about each other's feelings and successes."

 BI Performance Services in Minneapolis, Minnesota, holds a "good News Hour" every month. All available employees are invited at the beginning of the day to gather together and share good news, about the company, the world, and their personal lives. Employees love this time of sharing, and it definitely contributes to creating an atmosphere of appreciation.

TIPS FOR IMPLEMENTATION:

You will be surprised when you start this tradition in your organization how much people will love it. It should always be done informally, allowing and encouraging anyone in the organization to speak. The only difficulty is time, so it is good to set a limit up front. People at Kaset even created a "Wallow" banner to display during the sharing time!

Hold a Company-Wide Appreciation Day

THE IDEA:

Having a special day once or twice a year to honor the entire company is a great morale booster and helps to create company legends.

THE IDEA IN ACTION:

Mosby-Year Book, Inc., in St. Louis, Missouri, holds a company-wide Appreciation Day every September. Each of their 10 locations closes the company on any day they choose in September and holds a two to three hour event. It's usually a food and entertainment event, although one location chose to attend a baseball game one year and another goes on a riverboat cruise. At this event they give out Star Performer Awards. This is a peer award created by Gretchen Jaspering, Director of Communications and External Resources, nine years ago and she says, "It's easily the most popular award in the company." Peers nominate each other, and then a committee of peers throughout the company select the winners—about two percent to three percent of the employee population. The award is a brass star engraved with the winner's names and a check for $250. Gretchen says, "Not only is the award popular, but a place on the committee and the committee chairmanship are coveted as well."

I loved receiving a copy of a beautiful brochure that was titled "Mosby Stars" and the cover said:

On Appreciation Day each year Mosby employees, chosen by their colleagues, are honored with a STAR PERFORMER AWARD. To find out how these folks stand out from the crowd, the communications department asked them four questions:

- What did you accomplish this year that you are most proud of?
- What did you find the most challenging over the past year?

- Why is peer recognition so important?
- What advice would you give to someone just starting out in the publishing business?

Their answers reveal the spirit of the award which was created to recognize outstanding performance.

The brochure contains their pictures and a quotation from each of them. When asked what advice they would give, the number one answer was to find out as much as you can about the job you're doing and what the company does. Many confided that passing their knowledge along to others was important to them as well as being patient, flexible, and organized. It is a wonderful testimonial to others in the organization striving for this award.

Gretchen also shared that they have, as other companies do, committees and task forces for which employees volunteer that have nothing to do with their direct job responsibilities. At the end of each year, she compiles a list of those employees and they select a small gift—such as a pen, an umbrella, or a tote bag—to give to them. They give the gifts to the chairperson of each committee to give to the members and include a letter from the chairman of the company that thanks them and encourages them to continue.

TIPS FOR IMPLEMENTATION:

It is important to plan events that fit into your company's culture but also stretch now and then to surprise and delight your employees. Make sure that they are represented in the planning so there is buy-in, and it is truly received as "appreciation" and not "another boring company thing I have to go to!"

Notes

1. Van Warner, Rick. 1994. "A little praise goes a long way in keeping employees on the job." *Nation's Restaurant News*, 26 September, p. 19.

2. Glanz, Barbara A. 1993. *The Creative Communicator: 399 Tools to Communicate Commitment without Boring People to Death!* Burr Ridge, IL: Irwin Professional Publishing.

Personal Action Ideas

Write your ideas here!

Respect

A true leader is one who designs the cathedral and then shares the vision that inspires others to build it.

Jan Carlzon
Moments of Truth

CHAPTER

VI

R = RESPECT

Good management is largely a matter of love. Or if you're uncomfortable with that word, call it caring, because proper management involves caring for people, not manipulating them.

JAMES AUTRY
Love and Profit—The Art of Caring Leadership

"Value Each Individual in the Workplace"

People in today's world are starving for respect. They are tired of being treated like a number, and technology is only increasing the tendency to become one's social security, account, or employee number to the exclusion of our humanness.

I recently had an encounter in which I had a horrible experience with a credit card. When I called the customer service number of the company and shared this very emotional and traumatic experience, the first reply from the mouth of the employee was, "What's your account number?" In that one statement she completely disregarded my humanness and relegated me to simply being another number. There was no acknowledgment at all of my feelings. I ended up canceling my account because I no longer want to deal with organizations who do not care about me as a HUMAN being.

"Human resources."

So, too, do employees want to be considered as human beings in their places of work. They want to be appreciated, and they want to have a feeling of "being in on things." These involve respect and trust, a feeling that every person is an important part of the organization, and this respect and trust begin in each one-on-one interaction that occurs in the workplace.

Hyler Bracey, the author of *Managing from the Heart*, says employees basically want three things:

- Meaningful work
- A chance to impact decisions that affect them
- Good relationships

Hyler's organization, The Atlanta Consulting Group, has been doing some unique and powerful studies on trust in the workplace and its impact on organizational success. The following is an excerpt from his new book *Be Quick or Die*:

Lack of trust is ultimately lethal. An organization lacking it is eventually going to be dead in the water. But the good news is that lack of trust can be cured. Trust can be built by an organization by scrupulously underscoring trustworthy policies: telling the truth all the time, keeping agreements, and making sure everyone stays well-informed. Individuals also have a large role to play in trust building.

Our model of trust is a temple with four pillars: Openness, Honesty, Credibility, and Respect, undergirded by the need for Consistency.

Openness means sharing one's thoughts and feelings and being receptive to the same in others. It's self-disclosure as opposed to guardedness. As that openness is reciprocated, the trust level in the relationship is nudged higher.

Honesty, as used here, means giving truthful, complete feedback to others, for better or worse. "Feedback," says Ken Blanchard, co-author of *The One-Minute Manager* and other motivational books, "is the breakfast of champions." People want and need to know how they are doing.

Credibility means making and keeping agreements. You do so by (1) making only those agreements you intend to keep; (2) avoid making, or accepting, unclear or fuzzy agreements; (3) give early notice if an agreement must be broken; and (4) if you *must* break an agreement, make sure you initiate the renegotiation and try to mend your chipped credibility.

Respect means honoring five unspoken requests that people make of each other in any relationship. They are:

1. Listen non-judgmentally.
2. Acknowledge differences without assigning blame.
3. Give credit to others for their unique and special qualities.
4. Look for positive intentions.
5. Tell others your truth compassionately.

If you honor all five unspoken requests, the other person will consistently feel respected, even cared about.

When you are able to employ all four pillars—openness, honesty, credibility, and respect—your relationships will tend to be high-trust ones.

When all the employees of an organization follow suit—with sponsorship and role models offered by management—the corporate culture gains the critical competitive advantage of everyone working together to create a successful enterprise. This is a powerful medicine for any organization.

Riane Eisler, who founded the Center for Partnership Studies in Malibu, California, asserts that organizations based on a rigid, hierarchical, dictatorial management style are fast becoming a thing of the past in view of today's need for flexibility, customer service, and people-oriented philosophies. She describes two models of interaction: the "partnership" model and the "dominator" model. There are many different ways of achieving partnership, she says, but central is "a respect for the input and contributions" of all people. "The leader has a different function (in a partnership); it's an empowerment model, which elicits the best in people. And it's voluntary, not coercive."[1]

Ask yourself the questions, "Am I a spirit-regenerating leader? Do I demonstrate respect for the people in my workplace regardless of their position or rank?" No matter what your job in an organization is, you can begin to create a new level of trust in your daily interactions. As people feel more respected and valued in their places of work, they will perform from their hearts as well as from their heads.

Part One:

MAKE THE WORKPLACE A COMMUNITY

"The Price Is Right"

THE IDEA:

In order to help your employees feel commitment to the organization, it is important to give them as much financial information as possible. Some organizations do this through "Open Book Management," allowing all employees access to all the financial data of the company and even training them to be able to understand and interpret it. Other organizations encourage employees to work directly with vendors to help ensure getting the best prices. Information is power, and as information is shared, the power, too, is distributed in a way that makes employees feel important.

THE IDEA IN ACTION:

John Giattino, CHA, the General Manager of the Clarion Hotel in Virginia Beach, Virginia, wants a hotel with 115 owners! He has devised a creative way to help his associates value the property of the hotel. Once a month at their general pep rally and coffee break where they do such things as celebrate employees' birthdays with a special cake, each department takes a turn at playing "The Price Is Right." Items from the hotel inventory such as a pen, shampoo, a ream of copy paper, a vacuum, and a uniform top are placed on a table with the price of the hotel's cost facing down.

The members of the chosen department then guess what the hotel must pay for each item. The winners of each round receive $5 and then get to compete in a showcase. This might consist of pricing the cost of a full set of room amenities, and that winner gets a prize like two tickets to Busch Gardens. Mr. Giattino feels that if his associates understand the value of items they work with daily, they will respond as if they are the hotel owners, with respect and care. And the game adds fun and friendly competition to the workplace!

Employees at Southwest Airlines can win free trips by answering quizzes on business expenses in the quarterly newsletter. Their "Vice President of People," Ann Rhoades, says they are not concerned about where the employees get the answers. They just want them to understand business costs.[2]

TIPS FOR IMPLEMENTATION:

No matter what your business is, this idea is applicable. What a creative and fun way to share power and to "whack" people's thinking as consumers themselves! Be sure to include the most mundane items everyone in the organization uses daily.

Have a Special Day for All Employees

THE IDEA:

Honoring employees with a special day is a wonderful morale booster. It shows respect for them because the organization is willing to invest time and money in providing a valuable and unique experience focused on them.

THE IDEA IN ACTION:

Artex International in Highland, Illinois, recently held a quality rally at a beautiful location called Diamond Mineral Springs on a Saturday morning. The day was special because of several things:

- It began with the owners of the company doing a hilarious skit poking fun at themselves.
- They invited me to come to speak to the employees on regenerating the spirit in their workplace, and it was the first time plant people had ever had the opportunity of hearing a motivational speaker.
- Problem-solving quality teams from all parts of the company presented wonderfully funny, creative skits about actual work problems that had been solved.
- They were treated to an extraordinary lunch of barbecue, fried chicken, corn on the cob, and beer and soda.
- Employees were even bused back and forth to the main office so they could truly enjoy the day!

TIPS FOR IMPLEMENTATION:

Whenever possible, hold these days offsite. Involve employees in the planning so that you can be sure that the day will be valuable for THEM. Make the day voluntary so that those who hate social gatherings won't be forced to come and drag others down. The challenge is to make the day so exciting that no one will want to miss it!

Establish a Code of Conduct

THE IDEA:

Whenever you are a part of an ongoing team, committee, or other group that will be working together for a prolonged length of time, it is crucial to the effectiveness of the team to establish a Code of Conduct, listing the specific behaviors you will use in interacting with one another. It is also critical that each member of the team participate and agree on the final version. I even suggest having each member sign the Code and posting it in their regular meeting room or central work area as a reminder of their commitment.

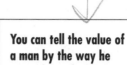

> **You can tell the value of a man by the way he treats his wife, by the way he treats a subordinate, and by the way he treats someone who can do nothing for him.**
>
> **KEN BABCOCK**
> *Superior Environmental Corporation*

THE IDEA IN ACTION:

I spent two days working with the training team of the Switching Systems Division of Rockwell International. As a part of this work, they created their team Code of Conduct:

- Be on time for all meetings
  Have an agenda with time limitations
  Stick to agenda/time frames
  Assign meeting roles

- Communication process
  State problems (feelings/facts)
  Possible solutions
  Your recommendations

- Time limit for floor
  OK to shelve topic
  Everyone speaks
  Individual responsibility
  Try time limit up front
- Leave personal disagreements aside.
- Listen when others talk.
- Be open with concerns.
- Treat everyone with professional respect.
- KEEP THE SLATE CLEAN.
- Do not say anything negative or unkind about the training delivery team.
- Share recognition of something not there that is needed—what is impacting customers.
- SHARE WHAT HAS BEEN DONE WELL (2–5 TIMES MORE).
- DEMONSTRATE LOYALTY.
- Share information with all team members—FYI.
- Evaluate ideas, not people.
- Practice positive intent.
- Focus on the situation, not the individual.

Their manager shared with me that the morale of the team has been much higher, that meetings have become much more pleasant and efficient, there is a new spirit of creativity and fun in the workplace, and that they are truly beginning to function as a team. They have decided to begin each meeting with "Hurrah" time and have even come up with a reminder to keep them on track with the behaviors in the code—when someone is not following the behaviors, they use the phrase "CHECK YOUR CODE!" They are even thinking about having buttons made with this slogan.

 The customer service team at Viscosity Oil in Willowbrook, Illinois, established this code of conduct, each individual signed it, and posted it in their common workspace:

- If someone has a problem with another person, come directly to that person.
- Don't put your finger in someone else's face.
- No back stabbing—don't say negative things about anyone.
- If someone comes to you with a problem, don't share that with others.
- Everyone come to work with a smile and KEEP IT!

TIPS FOR IMPLEMENTATION:

It is best to have an outside facilitator lead this process because it can be an emotional one, and a strong trust level must be developed to allow people to express deep feelings and concerns and to be honest in expressing the behaviors they desire in a working relationship. This often involves leaving "old baggage" behind and starting anew in these relationships, so it is crucial that *every member of the team* commits fully to these behaviors as the guide for how they will work together in the future.

Create a Human-Level Database

THE IDEA:

Companies have databases on employees that contain business-level information—education, previous experience, training, etc. I suggest that you create a database that contains interesting things about your staff on the human level.

THE IDEA IN ACTION:

Collect information about all employees such as:

- Special hobbies such as woodworking, furniture refinishing, crafts, cooking

- Special interests such as bridge, golf, theater, or horseback riding
- Do they speak another language?
- Do they play a musical instrument or sing?
- Do they like to draw or cartoon?
- Books, movies, and music that they like
- Favorite sports
- Organizations and support groups to which they belong
- Any other significant life experiences

You might even want to include spouses' hobbies and interests.

TIPS FOR IMPLEMENTATION:
This becomes a terrific way to network internally. From this data can spring informal internal classes (sharing their hobbies and interests), travel groups, and even a company chorus or band. People can find others to help them out with problems both at work and at home, and the company will discover resources it never knew it had. Best of all, employees are considered as whole persons, not just as workers!

Give People Special Tools of Importance

THE IDEA:
When you find employees reluctant to do certain tasks, it often helps to give them wonderful, classy tools to use, and then they become excited about doing the tasks because you have made them feel important.

THE IDEA IN ACTION:
My friend Dimitris Tsitos, the president of Synolic Quality Systems in Athens, Greece, told me of an experience he had with the second

largest enterprise in its field in Greece. The salesmen at the time were not eager to write reports, saying that their jobs were to sell, not to write. The General Manager of the company approved of Dimitris' suggestion for improving the situation, since the behavior of the sales reps was creating problems for the company. Dimitris said, "We bought for each sales rep an expensive (Mont Blanc) ball point, individualized with their name, and a luxurious leather folder/notebook for the reports. We presented them and asked them to use these at the same time we introduced the motto, 'Don't say it, Write it.' The results were absolutely satisfying!"

> Treat people as though they were what they ought to be and you help them become what they are capable of being.
>
> GOETHE

TIPS FOR IMPLEMENTATION:

Although your organization may not be able to afford Mont Blanc pens, look for the classiest thing you can afford. Your employees will be thrilled and will be much more apt to do the necessary work if they are proud of the tools with which to do it.

Treat Every Employee as a Manager

THE IDEA:

Karl Albrecht in his book, At America's Service writes:

> This is a provocative concept; every service employee is a manager, in a way. Each one controls the outcome of the moment of truth by having control over his or her own behavior toward the customer. If service people are apathetic, disagreeable, unfriendly, cold, distant, or uncooperative, their moments of truth go to hell in a handbasket. If they are lively, pleasant, warm, friendly, cooperative, and resourceful in taking care of the customer's problem, then their

"Now then, does anyone else have an opinion on my proposal?"

moments of truth shine, and the customer tends to generalize those experiences to your overall service image. It may be a frightening prospect for some managers: The ant army is in charge.[3]

When employees understand this concept and realize that they, in fact, ARE managers, it boosts their self-esteem and feelings of importance about their jobs. In our society, the designation of "manager" connotes importance and value.

THE IDEA IN ACTION:

A branch office manager in the Michigan Department of State has decided to put the word "Manager" after each staff member's name on their lockers and drawers. At Bachrach Clothing in Decatur, Illinois, they gave everyone buttons that say, "I'M A MANAGER!"

 Do all your employees have business cards, the symbol of success in today's world? I suggest that organizations give every single employee their own business cards with the title of "Manager of Moments of Truth." Perhaps these can be a reward or thank you for their one-year anniversary if your organization experiences a lot of turnover, but imagine the difference in morale and self-esteem if employees really felt like managers!

TIPS FOR IMPLEMENTATION:

Business cards can be readily and inexpensively made on computers if you don't have the budget to have them printed. Just remember that if you can instill in your employees that they ARE managers and treat them that way, they will have a new commitment to their very important jobs!

> "For six months now, I've been visiting the workplaces of America, administering a simple test. I call it the "pronoun test." I ask front-line workers a few general questions about the company. If the answers I get back describe the company in terms like "they" and "them," then I know it's one kind of a company. If the answers are put in terms like "we" or "us," I know it's a different kind of company.
>
> SECRETARY OF LABOR ROBERT B. REICH

Trust Employees

THE IDEA:

A great part of respecting employees is trusting them to do their best and to do what is right. Like the self-fulfilling prophecy, employees will probably live up to the expectations of their management! In a command and control, policed environment, there is little incentive for the values of trust and respect.

THE IDEA IN ACTION:

In his book *Managing by Storying Around*, David Armstrong tells of ways they treat their employees with respect. In a new shop the organization had just acquired, the managers decided to remove the time clock to show the employees how Armstrong did things. "If we really believe that our people are our strongest asset, then we should treat them as if they are," the managers said. "Why should we have a time clock that humiliates them? They're adults. They know what time they are supposed to be at work. They know what's expected of them." The managers showed through their actions that they believed the people they worked with were trustworthy and important. The moral of the story according to Armstrong:

> *Treat people like people. Life is easier, and you are more productive in the long term if you show respect for the people who work for you. A 'do it or else' attitude works only in the short term.*[4]

The company cafeteria at Armstrong is run completely on the honor system. The vending machines are unlocked, there is no cash register, and the employees pay for their food by putting money into an open coin box. Armstrong says, "Either you trust your employees or you don't. If you trust them, you don't need locked cash registers, time clocks, and scores of supervisors. If you don't trust them, get rid of them."[5]

TIPS FOR IMPLEMENTATION:

I apply these principles when I give workshops and presentations. I set up a table with all my books, audio tapes, and videotapes in the back of the room or even out in the hall, and I simply leave a price list and an open cash box with change in it for as long as I'm there. I truly believe that if we trust people, most of them will honor that trust. It may shock your employees if you begin giving them too much control too quickly, so do it gradually until they see that you really do trust them. You are telling people that you believe in them, and that faith will be rewarded in positive morale, renewed creativity, and increased productivity.

Balance of Work and Family

The revolution is on toward shared roles in work and family. The new flexibility is humanizing the workplace, bringing more balance to employees' lives and boosting corporate productivity.

Part Two:

BRINGING THE TWO HALVES OF YOUR LIFE TOGETHER—BALANCING WORK AND FAMILY

Bonnie Michaels, the President of Managing Work & Family, Inc., in Evanston, Illinois, writes:

> Being family-friendly doesn't necessarily mean child care centers or big budgets. Most employees want understanding and acceptance from co-workers and supervisors. They want to work in an environment where they can have flexibility for those days when children or elders are sick. Or, if there is a school conference or a special event, they would like to negotiate to have the flexibility to attend these family functions. There are many little things that make the environment one that is caring, especially respect for one another's lifestyle choices—singlehood; married, with/without children; single parents; blended families. Employees especially need support from co-workers to stand in or trade schedules for family/personal emergencies. This support can be paid back by opting to help that co-worker when their special needs arise.

She lists a number of ideas that work:

1. Beepers for expectant Dads are provided by L.A. Water and Power.

2. Portable breast pumps are provided by Amoco Corporation for returning Moms who want to continue nursing.

3. Concierge services at Anderson Consulting help employees with everyday assistance such as laundry, dry-cleaning, and gift giving.

4. A nursing room is provided by Hewitt Associates to allow women returning from maternity leave to continue to nurse.

5. Many companies provide space and flyers for support groups such as single parents and elder care.

6. Caregiver Fairs are events sponsored by companies such as First National Bank of Chicago. They bring in local resources to exhibit and help employees with health and family issues.

7. At TRW an employee's wife became ill and sadly died. They had young children. The employee's co-workers donated some of their personal vacation time to this individual so that he could stay home on an extended leave with his children and still receive full compensation.

Family-Oriented Employee Benefits

THE IDEA:

Anytime the organization can help the employee to balance the demands of work and family, the reward will be happier, more productive employees, and everyone will win.

THE IDEA IN ACTION:

The MetroWest section of the *Chicago Tribune*, August 9, 1995, contained an article about Fel-Pro, a manufacturer of gaskets, sealants, and lubricants for the auto and industrial markets. For eight weeks each summer, the children of hundreds of Fel-Pro employees go to a company-sponsored day camp while their parents begin another day of work.

At the Skokie-based company, the children board company-provided buses for the hour ride to the company-owned camp, which has been in existence for the last 22 years. The camp is on 220 acres dotted with hills, nature trails, swimming pools, stocked lakes and facilities for golf, frisbee, and soccer. This summer 215 children attended the camp, and the facilities are also available to the 2000 company employees on weekends. The camp was started as a result of employee concerns about the lack of supervised, daily activities in the summer for school-aged children. David Weinberg, co-chairman of the company and a grandson of one of its founders, says, "Where we might have had an employee who was anxious or nervous (about their children), we now have an employee who can focus fully on his or her job."

Fel-Pro has other child-oriented benefits as well: a program that starts before the child's birth with on-site prenatal classes for parents; every employee's child receives a $1,000 savings bond at birth payable on his or her 21st birthday; $5,000 to help defray adoption costs; on-site daycare; at-home sick child care; tutoring; college counseling; and $3,000 to help defray college costs. As a result, there is little turnover at Fel-Pro. David Weinberg believes if you treat your workers well and address their personal concerns, they will be happier and more productive, and the company will benefit as well. He says, "It's so much more fun to come to work under these conditions!"[6]

 I recently received a letter from Gretchen Jaspering, the Director of Communications and External Relations for Mosby-Year Book, Inc., in St. Louis, Missouri. She writes:

> As I sit here at work on a Sunday afternoon, I'm reminded of why I'm here as well as how fortunate I am to work for Mosby. I had to stay home with a sick child two days this week. Mosby allows us to use our sick days for our children and other sick family members. I didn't have to come in today to make up the time, but I did anyway because I like my job at Mosby and feel like I owe it to the company. For me, the flexibility we provide to employees is a big part of providing the kind of spirited workplace you describe.

TIPS FOR IMPLEMENTATION:

Although your organization may not be able to provide the extensive benefits of Fel-Pro, begin wherever you are able. Most importantly, ask your employees what THEY would like. At Fel-Pro most of the benefits have come from employee urging or a direct response to employee concerns.

Sponsor a Family Day at Work

THE IDEA:

One of the best ways to promote a better understanding of parent's jobs is to provide a day for families to come to work and learn more about what goes on there.

THE IDEA IN ACTION:

The American Hospital Association holds a "Day for Play at Work" celebration annually for families of employees with games, stations, prizes, and a tour of Mom's/Dad's workspace. It is designed to teach children just what it means to go to work. "To children, 'work' is an abstract place," says Bonnie Michaels, President of Managing Work & Family, Inc. "When they see for themselves where their parents work, how long it takes to get there, who they work with, and what they do all day, it creates a better understanding. Family days give children a positive feeling about their parents' work."

Activities have included making a "memory button" of the day, creating a "family album" of what kind of work each member of the family does, having a Polaroid family portrait taken in the work environment, and playing with typewriters, phones, computers, and other office equipment. "Family day gives employers the chance to boost morale and show employees that the company really cares about them as family people as well as workers," says Michaels.[7]

The DMV in Virginia sponsored a contest asking children and grandchildren of employees to draw a picture of what they thought their Mom/Dad/Grandmother/Grandfather did at work all day. These were framed and hung throughout the lobby of the building. The customers loved it, and the children were thrilled to come and see their pictures![8]

It is hard to believe, but the U.S. Navy, according to Deb Kraus of Lansing, Michigan, does something even more dramatic to improve the morale of their new recruits. The parents are invited to go on a seven-day cruise from Honolulu to Alameda, California, aboard the aircraft carrier on which their child is stationed. The purpose of the visit is for the parents to see what their son or daughter is doing, to experience life on board the ship, and also to help combat the homesickness of many of the recruits.

The Kraus' son, Shawn, is stationed on board the USS Abraham Lincoln, the navy's newest ship, as a cook. Deb and her husband, for a very minimal fee, were able to spend a week with their son, 1400 other civilians (parents or guardians), and 4000 naval personnel. They had tours of the ship, learned about all aspects of their son's job as well as other job duties on the ship, and even got to work with Shawn in the kitchen!

Deb says that by the third day, after cold showers, getting up at 6:00 AM, sleeping in a bunk bed three tiers high, and sharing a bathroom with 100 other women, she really empathized with her son's new lifestyle. She not only respects him more because of the limitations of this chosen career, but she also said, "My #1 priority in the future is that when that ship is out to sea, Shawn will get a card or letter every single day." What a very special way to improve morale as well as parent/child relationships!

Other organizations sponsor days when employees bring their children to work, and there are a variety of activities according to the ages of the children. A training company let older children experience being in the classes that their parents either trained, developed, or sold. Younger children were given tasks to perform to "help" such as copying and delivering mail. They all got to have their choice of food in the company cafeteria and make at least one phone call from their parent's desk! The young guests ended the day by creating flip charts about what they had learned and receiving certificates for their participation.

TIPS FOR IMPLEMENTATION:

You may want to begin this spirit regenerator with a short function such as an open house; however, when a family member can truly experience the feeling of the workplace, they will feel much more committed to support the employee when they are in a crisis and must give inordinate amounts of time to the job. When this does happen, the employer or manager can REWARD THE FAMILY AT HOME, thanking them for "sharing" their family member and assuring them that this is only a temporary situation.

Plan a Family Party

THE IDEA:

One of the best ways to improve communication in an organization is to have a party! A special, shared event can enhance communication between various locations, between management and employees, and between work and family.

THE IDEA IN ACTION:

My special friend Cheryl Regan, the president of the Learning Curve in Auckland, New Zealand, tells of her work with Pharmaceutical Sales and Marketing, Ltd., in New Zealand:

The company has four factories, each with a very different culture. You have to understand that each plant has different management, different styles, and they have not really talked to one another. So they have people of all cultures, all different thinking styles, and different religions who have never had the chance to communicate.

We decided that to get teamwork going, we would plan a huge party. The HR manager and I went out to all the plants and got them into teams and asked them to draft out what *they* wanted during the day. We took them through some brainstorming skills and had fun mind mapping their ideas for the day of celebration.

Once we came up with a structure for the day, we then had cross-functional teams working together from the various plants. The food team organized the food for all cultures; the game team had to think of games for the whole day. They had pie throwing, children's games, clowns, face painting, etc. Santa Claus came pulled in on Cydesdale horses. I played the elf!

All families were invited. Each department in every plant put up a display of what they did at work so that everyone in all the plants as well as their family members would know what was happening in each factory. It ended up with about 1000 people showing up!

From this day, everyone started to get to know each other. There is teamwork going on within the factories now, and facilitation skills, coaching, and counseling skills are being taught in-house. They have a ways to go yet, but the spirit of the P.S.M. family day started them on their journey!

TIPS FOR IMPLEMENTATION:

One of the keys to this venture's success was to have cross-teams of employees participate in the planning. A second wise decision was including the employees' families. A social event with support from employees and families included will always create a new spirit of respect and teamwork in an organization.

Part Three:

PERSONAL EXECUTIVE ACTIONS: SPECIAL THINGS TOP MANAGERS CAN DO TO MAKE PEOPLE FEEL IMPORTANT

Give Partners a Share in the Company's Success

THE IDEA:

Giving employees an opportunity to share financially in the success of the company not only creates a feeling of partnership but also gives them much more pride in the organization.

THE IDEA IN ACTION:

Jack Kahl, the president of Manco in Westlake, Ohio, sold some of his stock in 1985 to an ESOP so that his employees could own 30 percent of the company while he retained 70 percent. No longer just employees but co-owners, they became known as "partners" instead. Every partner is eligible for the ESOP after being employed for 60 days and is 100 percent vested after five years with Manco. Darla Ward, Sales Administrator at Manco says, "For our partners, Manco is now not only a place to come to work, but *their* place to come to work. As such, it's in their own best interest always to go the extra mile to do the right thing for customers. While customer service has always been important here, it's been heightened so much by people owning a 'piece of the rock.'"

Jack Kahl also believes in giving partners a voice and keeping them informed. Once a month everyone is invited to an ESOP meeting where information is shared about the financial status of the company, including profits and sales made, the direction the company is going, and plans for keeping it on track. The partners are truly treated like partners in the fullest sense.

TIPS FOR IMPLEMENTATION:

Perhaps sharing company ownership through stock is not possible in your organization, but think of other ways to create "ownership"—bonuses, profit sharing, or even job titles.

Communicate with All Levels in the Organization

THE IDEA:

A study by the Gordon Group, Inc., for the California Public Employees' Retirement System found: "Companies that involve employees more often in decision-making boast stronger market valuations than those that don't."[9] In order to create a feeling of respect throughout the organization, it is vital for the person running the company to really LISTEN to his or her employees at all levels. To be most effective, this should be a regularly scheduled process.

THE IDEA IN ACTION:

 USAir's Chairman and CEO, Seth E. Schofield, has created an Ambassadors group, his personal communication link to what is "really going on out there." Work group representatives from a variety of locations throughout the company, worldwide, get together with Mr. Schofield once every second month to discuss issues relating to the company and their respective work areas. They are nonmanagement employees representing customer services, flight attendants, ramp services, maintenance, reservations, pilots, and other such departments.

These employees express diverse viewpoints about the company. Mr. Schofield listens, offers his comments, provides updates on current events and issues at USAir, and then follows up with the group on events and issues from the previous month's meeting. These ambassadors serve a term of at least one year and are nominated by their peers, former Ambassadors, managers, supervisors, and other senior members of their departments. Mr. Schofield reviews the nominees and makes the final selections.

 Another CEO with whom I've worked makes what he calls "Whistle Stop" tours where he regularly visits different offices and branches of his company. These are informal visits that he uses to ask employees at all levels, "What do you like best about working here?" and "What are two things you would change about our company or your job if you had complete power to do so?" He then sends the branch or office a letter after his visit to let them know actions he has taken as a result of their suggestions.

TIPS FOR IMPLEMENTATION:

This kind of communication vehicle to encourage feedback from all levels will only be as valuable as the senior person allows it to be. If he or she is truly open to concerns and ideas from the front lines and most importantly ACTS on these concerns and ideas, then the process will be one of great value with everyone feeling a sense of participation. If, however, this is a "token" meeting and little or no action is taken regarding the feedback, it will soon become another political "feel good" session for upper management.

Empower Your Employees

THE IDEA IN ACTION:

Denise Raver, a former consultant for Performance Systems Corporation in Dallas, Texas, wrote me about the following example of empowerment:

> After reading Eric Harvey and Al Lucia's book *Walk the Talk*, Hank Gallina, Special Projects Administrator for the Lompoc Unified School District, decided that it was rather absurd that he sign each and every requisition for office supplies. He therefore empowered his two-office staff to sign requisitions themselves. He said it was as if he told them that they could each have two *additional* weeks of vacation—they were that impressed with this new authority. Do you know that they spent less money on office supplies than they had in years past?

TIPS FOR IMPLEMENTATION:

Nothing shows respect more than allowing people to be empowered to use their own best judgment. However, make sure that along with the permission you also give them protection when they goof. Use those goofs or mistakes as coaching opportunities, not as times to beat up on the employee. The first time they goof and the way you handle it will determine if they ever risk making an empowered decision again.

Poke Fun at Yourself

THE IDEA:

Anytime you can comfortably be a little bit silly and not take yourself too seriously it gives others permission not to be perfect and to laugh at themselves as well. This is especially true of supervisors

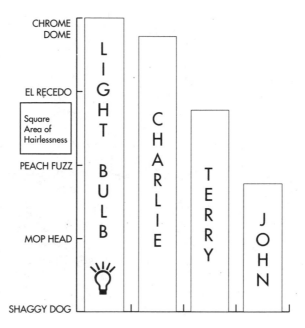

and managers. When they "lighten up," it allows everyone the chance to have more fun at work.

THE IDEA IN ACTION:

When Artex International held their first quality rally, part of the program was a group of skits written and performed by quality improvement teams from across the company. The beginning skit, however, was a big surprise—the Anderson brothers, the owners of the company, presented their own skit. Since all of them, including their father, the founder of the company, are in varying stages of hair loss, they tackled the problem of hairlessness from a Total Quality perspective.

They began with a FLOW CHART: "Is there hair?" that traced the roots of their hairlessness from "Birth" to "No Hair" to "The End." Next came a graph that showed the progression from "Hair " to "Peach Fuzz" to "No Hair" by their age in decades. They then did a bar graph of the "Square Area of Hairlessness" for each, going from bottom to top (Shaggy Dog—Mop Head—Peach Fuzz—El Recedo—Chrome Dome).

Finally, as their finale, they each appeared with a process solution—one with a rainbow-colored clown wig, one with a straw hat, and the youngest with a Banana Republic paper bag over his head with a picture of a monkey instead of his face! The employees LOVED the skit. Their most senior managers not only poked fun at themselves, but they also used the quality improvement tools in a way that NO ONE at Artex will ever forget!

Jack Kahl, the president of Manco in Westlake, Ohio, promised in 1990 that if sales reached the company's goal that year, he would swim across the lake by Manco's offices. In October, when sales surpassed the goal, he jumped in wearing swim trunks that read "the $60 Million Plunge." Not only has this swim become an annual event, but now others are participating as well!

TIPS FOR IMPLEMENTATION:

Never ever force anyone to take part in this fun unless they choose to. However, when you take the risk to be human, you open many doors for more honest, trusting, comfortable, and creative relationships to occur.

Emphasize the Value of the WHOLE Employee

THE IDEA:

The senior leaders have a great deal of influence on how much spirit exists in an organization. If they support a family atmosphere and recognize the needs of the whole employee, then they make it much easier for individuals to make that spirit come alive.

THE IDEA IN ACTION:

Guy Shoenecker, the President and Chief Quality Officer of BI Performance Services in Minneapolis, Minnesota, is deeply committed to the "BI Family" and the company's consideration for the whole employee—intellectual, skills, health, family, and spiritual. To promote this feeling, Guy personally greets all visitors and new employees. He describes himself as a "servant-leader, cheerleading the team." He makes it a point to always be at occasions when his employees need him, such as visiting them in the hospital and attending funerals. He greets them weekly on the loudspeaker with "Hi! This is Guy," sharing information with the entire company, and often stands at the door and shakes hands with many of the 1100+ employees as they come to work in the morning.

The company is founded on Christian values, and these are emphasized through respect, collaboration, and a commitment to the value of every individual. As a result, there are no job descriptions at BI, only accountabilities; associates do their own self-evaluation as an important part of their performance review; there is no private parking to separate people; titles are nearly non-existent; and even the executive offices are very plain. Open communication is encouraged throughout the organization. In fact, employees are encouraged to become "DWeeBS" (Dumb- Work Busters)!

Right relationships built on respect result in regenerated spirits which, in turn, impact the bottom line. In 1994, BI was the first service company to win the Minnesota Quality Award.

TIPS FOR IMPLEMENTATION:

Recognizing that human beings are your most valuable resource must exist in *actions*, not just in talk. When members of senior management personally demonstrate their commitment to the whole person, then others in the company will buy into the concept and make it a reality throughout the organization.

Show Your Employees that You Care

THE IDEA:

Find creative ways to show your employees often that you, the manager, really do care about them as individuals (both on the business and the human levels).

 Marge Rossiter, a former Sales Manager for First Chicago Bank in Downers Grove, Illinois, shares some of the things she did to show her employees that she cared:

1. Put candy in their mailboxes.

2. Had "ice cream" treats on occasion—only the best, Dove Bars!

3. Wrote notes of encouragement, especially when they had achieved a success of some sort or just thanking them for "hanging in there" when it was needed.

4. Left them voice mail messages telling them how great a department they were, especially in the morning to help them get a great start to their day.

5. Would take them out to lunch to discuss a problem (either work-related or personal) so that we could get away from the bank and have some relaxed time to share and solve or just "rap" about a situation.

6. Always got them gift certificates on holidays; candy at Halloween; in the summer bought them fresh peaches that were "ripened on the tree" ($1.79 per pound! but they were worth it!!!).

7. If a person was having a personal problem, I would "stay close" to let that person know I really cared. Many times my boss would "take me to task" for being too easy with that person. However, it paid off in the long run—my people were extremely devoted, loyal, and hardworking.

8. Took them out to breakfast as a group to celebrate a sales success.

9. Made sure I mentioned their sales successes to the boss.

10. Always let them know that I cared about them. I was never afraid to sign my cards "Love, Marge!"

TIPS FOR IMPLEMENTATION:

It is important to find ideas that you are personally comfortable with, but don't be afraid to get out of your comfort zone now and then. Sometimes when we try something new, we find that we really like it!

> **(A good manager is one who) approaches management as a calling, a life engagement that, if done properly, combines technical and administrative skills with vision, compassion, honesty, and trust to create an environment in which people can grow personally, can feel fulfilled, can contribute to a common good, and can share in the psychic and financial rewards of a job well done.**
>
> **JAMES A. AUTRY**
> *Love and Profit—The Art of Caring Leadership*

Notes

1. Butruille, Susan G. 1990. "Corporate Caretaking." *Training & Development Journal*, April, p. 53.

2. Allerton, Haidee. 1995. "Working Life—Cost-Effective Procedures." *Training & Development Journal*, March, p. 71.

3. Albrecht, Karl. 1988. At *America's Service*. Homewood, IL: Dow Jones-Irwin, p. 28.

4. Armstrong, David. 1992. *Managing by Storying Around: A New Method of Leadership*. New York, NY: Doubleday Currency, pp. 23–24.

5. Armstrong, David. 1992. *Managing by Storying Around: A New Method of Leadership*. New York, NY: Doubleday Currency, PP. 21–22.

6. Randle, Wilma. 1995. "Day camp is good business: Fel-Pro perk makes kids and workers productive in summer." *Chicago Tribune*, *Metro West*, Wednesday, 9 August, p. 1.

7. Editor. 1990. "In Practice: All Work and Some Play." *Training & Development Journal*, December, p. 9.

8. Glanz, Barbara A. 1993. *The Creative Communicator: 399 Tools to Communicate Commitment without Boring People to Death!* Burr Ridge, IL: Irwin Professional Publishing, p. 77.

9. Mitchell, Russell & Omeal, Michael. 1994. "Managing by Values." *BusinessWeek*, 1 August, p. 47.

Personal Action Ideas

Write your ideas here!

Reason for Being

Without work, all life turns rotten. But when work is soulless, life stifles and dies.

Albert Camus

CHAPTER VII

R = REASON FOR BEING

An unemployed existence is a worse negation of life than death itself. Because to live means to have something definite to do—a mission to fulfill—and in the measure in which we avoid setting our life to something, we make it empty... Human life, by its very nature, has to be dedicated to something.

JOSE ORTEGA Y GASSET

"You Are Not a Number! Find Your Own Special Purpose"

Because the old employment contract of always having a job if you were only loyal to the organization is now gone, workers must find a personal sense of mission or purpose in new ways. They must direct their own career, they must plan on several different jobs and perhaps even careers in a lifetime, and they must, as Tom Peters says, "Repot themselves every five years."

With all these changes in the workplace, changes in job descriptions, changes in technology occurring almost daily, and the need to become a lifelong learner, individuals must have an anchor to ground themselves. To be fully productive and happy, they must find a "reason for being." If the organization for which they work has a mission and a guiding set of values, the employee can buy into those or can choose to adjust his own purpose and values to exist in that organization. If the individual AND the organization, however, have no values or sense of purpose, the workplace will be sterile and without spirit.

Charles Garfield in his book *Peak Performers* tells the story of a group of people in an aerospace company in southern California who took care of the pipes in the building. They had the lowest turnover and the lowest absentee rate in the company, yet the president of the company asked, "How could you teach them peak performance? They're only plumbers!" When Garfield went to their department for a tour, he discovered they were all wearing surgical greens. When he questioned why, the supervisor said his son, who was a cardiovascular surgeon, had gotten them those scrubs, and just like his son took care of the pipes in the human body, they took care of the pipes in that organization, and there weren't going to be any heart attacks while THEY were in charge! They then went to the locker room where "Dr. _____" was stenciled on every locker. Why was turnover and absenteeism so low? THEY HAD A REASON FOR BEING![1]

> **You are not here merely to make a living. You are here to enable the world to live more amply, with greater vision, with a finer spirit of hope and achievement. You are here to enrich the world, and you impoverish yourself if you forget the errand.**
>
> **WOODROW WILSON**

Bob Greene tells in one of his newspaper columns how he spent a week with one of the Tribune employees delivering the papers at 3:00 am each morning, a job few of us would seek! When he questioned the young woman he was riding with as to what personal satisfaction she got from doing this job, she explained that she viewed it as "a Rumpelstiltskin deal." Each night when she arrived at the warehouse, there were huge piles of papers and inserts, and just like Rumpelstiltskin spun the huge piles of straw into gold, she sorted all those papers into neat individual packages and then delivered her "gold" to the people in each home who would be eagerly awaiting them the next morning. She, too, had a reason for being.[2]

"At the original release I related with the rebels. Now that I've climbed the corporate ladder I feel as if I've joined the Empire and am controlled by the Dark Force."

I recently heard about a cafeteria worker in an inner city junior high school. Again, a job most of us would avoid! When someone asked her why she liked her job, she replied that this was the only healthy, hot meal many of these children would get all day, and she wanted to serve it to them with love and care. She had a sense of purpose.

Do you have a meaningful purpose in what you do at work? If not, remember the three column chart from Chapter Two. Choosing to create a positive experience each time you interact with anyone can become your personal sense of mission. You are important, and YOU CAN MAKE A DIFFERENCE!

Create a Personal Mission Statement

THE IDEA:

Create a short statement that expresses who you are and what your work is. This is a statement of purpose and values to serve as a touchstone for all that you do.

THE IDEA IN ACTION:

Here is my personal mission statement:

> *I am here as the Lord's helper to "spread contagious enthusiasm"™ and to lovingly and creatively help other people and myself see the choices we have to make a difference in the world.*

My good friend, Ken Blanchard, who first challenged me to do a mission statement, gives this as his purpose:

> *To be a loving teacher and example of simple truths that help myself and others to awaken the presence of God in our lives.*

When Saint Francis Medical Center in Peoria, Illinois, created a 10½ by 7 foot mural as a symbol of its Vision, everyone had a part in painting it, so they all participated in the big picture. However, the workers in Food and Nutrition took this to heart in a more creative and personal way. They have written their own personal visions as a way to express their desire to give customers quality service and bring the Sisters' Mission to life in their daily work. Here are two of their personal visions:

> Liane Adams, Nutrition Assistant: *I have a very busy job processing diet orders and phone calls. I strive to achieve a balance of professionalism,*

positive attitude, a sense of humor, and a willingness to do whatever it takes to fulfill my obligations to the Health Care System and my office family.

Olivia McClintock, Trayline: **Kind words, helping hands, caring heart, striving to meet the needs of those in my care (my fellow employees, the patients, and their families). A true devotion to work that I have been doing.**

Saint Francis had the vision statements of all employees who created them printed on cards and laminated with their names on them.

TIPS FOR IMPLEMENTATION:

Work on this project over a period of time so that it really comes from your heart as well as from your head. Then memorize your mission statement and use it as an anchor in making hard decisions about your life and your career.

Add a Personal Signature to Your Work

THE IDEA:

This is a wonderful challenge for us all—what can we do to differentiate ourselves from all the other people who do the same work we do? In these days of career changing and layoffs, it becomes essential, I believe, that we strive to find a way to stand out from the crowd, to be special.

THE IDEA IN ACTION:

As a professional speaker, I have two personal signatures that differentiate me from other presenters. One is the "Pass It On"™

cards which I have given to over 16,000 people. The other is the atmosphere I create. No matter what size group I speak to, whether it is 30 or 3000, I line the walls of the room or ballroom with 50–60 brightly-colored, laminated flip charts with quotations in my hand-writing that relate to my speaking topic. My "customers" love it, it enhances learning, and it is memorable.

 A nurse leaves a handwritten card by the bedside of her patients with a note introducing herself and assuring them of her care and understanding.

 A United Airlines pilot, after he gets things under control in the cockpit, goes to the computer and randomly selects the names of several passengers. He then handwrites short notes to them, thanking them for their business. When the flight attendant delivers them, it is a delightful surprise for all!

 A Northwest Airlines baggage attendant collects name tags that fall off luggage, and instead of throwing them away as they used to do, he mails them back to their owners.

 A taxi driver gives his customers a choice of five different kinds of music on cassette tapes as well as a variety of that day's newspapers to read. He also has a mission statement: "To get his customers to their destination as quickly, as safely, and as comfortably as possible!"

 An auto mechanic puts his card in every car he repairs. It reads, "This car cared for by (his name)."

 Pastor Paul Wilcox of the First Methodist Church in Harlan, Iowa, spends a great deal of his time visiting church members who are ill or shut-ins. To add a special, memorable sparkle to his visits, he brings his harmonica along and plays for his parishioners. When my mother had surgery recently, the second day he visited he first played "How Great Thou Art" to thank God for the success of the surgery and then, as my mother said, "He played a 'jazzier' tune" to boost her spirits!

A vendor who owned a hot dog stand always asked the customer's name. His personal signature was to write their name in mustard on the hot dog!

 One of the most touching examples of adding a personal signature is what I call "The Johnny Story":

> Recently I was asked to speak to 3000 employees of a large supermarket chain in the Midwest, an experience which led to one of the most heartwarming blessings of my entire speaking career. In this presentation, I especially stressed the idea of adding a personal signature to your work.
>
> About three weeks after I had spoken to the supermarket employees, my phone rang late one afternoon. The person on the line told me that his name was Johnny and that he was a bagger in one of the stores. He also told me that he was a Down's Syndrome person. He said, "Barbara, I liked what you said!" Then he went on to tell me how when he'd gone home that night, he asked his Dad to teach him to use the computer.
>
> He said they set it up in three columns, and each night now when he goes home, he finds a "thought for the day." He said when he can't find one he likes, he "thinks one up!" Then he types it into the computer, prints them, cuts them out, and signs his name on the back of each one. The next day as he bags customer's groceries, "with flourish" **he puts a thought for the day in each person's groceries he bags**, adding his own personal signature in a heartwarming, fun, and creative way.
>
> One month later the manager of the store called me. He said, "Barbara, you won't believe what happened today. . . . When I went out on the floor this morning, the line at Johnny's checkout was *three times longer* than any other line!" He said, "I went ballistic, yelling, 'Get more lanes open! Get more people out here,' but the customers said, 'No no! We *want* to be in Johnny's lane—we want the thought for the day!'"
>
> He said one woman even came up and told him, "I only used to shop once a week, and now I come in every time I go

by because I want the thought for the day!" (Imagine what that does to the bottom line.) He ended by saying, "Who do you think is the **most important person** in our whole store?" Johnny, of course!

Three months later he called me again, "You and Johnny have transformed our store! Now in the floral department when they have a broken flower or an unused corsage, they go out on the floor and find an elderly woman or a little girl and pin it on them. One of our meat packers loves Snoopy, so he bought 50,000 Snoopy stickers, and each time he packages a piece of meat, he puts a Snoopy sticker on it. **We** are having so much fun, and our **customers** are having so much fun!" THAT is spirit in the workplace!

TIPS FOR IMPLEMENTATION:

It never ceases to amaze me whenever I tell this beautiful story how little it takes to regenerate the spirit in a workplace. Johnny took what many of us might consider to be a not very important job and he *made* it important by adding his own personal signature. My challenge and yours—*if young Johnny can do it, there is no reason why each one of us can't do it, too.* Imagine the new spirits of self-esteem, commitment, and fun that could permeate our places of work if we each, like Johnny, found a way to add our special, unique touch to our job!

Write a Song about a Company Hero or Legend

THE IDEA:

Writing a poem or a song about a company legendary story or a company hero captures the spirit forever. I believe that we are surrounded in every organization by unrecognized and unutilized talents that, if given support and permission, will blossom. Often encouragement and ideas are all that is needed to unlock the creativity inside a potential musician or writer.

THE IDEA IN ACTION:

I was deeply blessed to meet David Roth, a wonderfully talented songwriter and performer from Seattle, Washington, at the International Humor and Creativity Conference in April where we were both presenting. After experiencing his deeply sensitive words and music, I shared with him "The Johnny Story" in this book, hoping that he would create something that would be able to touch many lives on a different level from my writing and speaking. This is the song he has written to celebrate Johnny:

A Little Something More

I started him collecting carts and sweeping up the floor
In no time flat young Johnny was a bagger in my store
He took such pride and worked so hard it rubbed off on my
   crew
And just because he only did the best that he could do.

Chorus

Johnny is a bagger in our local grocery store
Packing people's food away as they go out the automatic door
Just a job ten thousand other people do
But Johnny found a way to make it new.

A couple weeks went by and I began to notice something
It started in the parking lot after people had done their shop-
   ping
They were digging through their groceries and coming out with
   smiles
I made a mental note and came inside to check the aisles.

The store was pretty busy, must be five o'clock, I guessed
And here the line in Johnny's lane was twice as long as all the rest

"No waiting on 1 through 4 . . . " I said, they didn't seem to care
"We want to be on Johnny's line . . . " they said, and stayed
  right there.

That's when I discovered Johnny's magic secret brainstorm
A little note he put in every shopper's bag before they went
  home
And every note had what he called his "thought" for that same
  day
And Johnny signed the back of each good thought he gave
  away.

Chorus

Johnny is a bagger in our local grocery store
Packing people's food away as they go out the automatic door
Just a job ten thousand other people do
But Johnny found a way to make it new.

Of course Johnny's got the longest lines of any shop in town
He's also got some syndrome that the doctors label "Down"
If you ask me how one person makes a difference any more
Come on by, see Johnny at our store.

Chorus

Johnny is a bagger in our local grocery store
Packing people's food away as they go out the automatic door
And he's making things a little better than they were before
The most important person in our store
Johnny always gives a little something more!

Reprinted with permission, Copyright 1995, David Roth

TIPS FOR IMPLEMENTATION:

Think about a story or hero in your organization. Then begin a
search for an "undiscovered" musician or writer to capture the special spirit of that story.

Have a Scavenger Hunt for New Employees

THE IDEA:

Use new employee orientation as a time to create a feeling of teamwork and customer service by organizing a scavenger hunt to find where things are located in the building.

THE IDEA IN ACTION:

Dolores Power, an RN from Holt, Michigan, shared her new employee experience:

> When I hired in, the first two days of orientation at Ingham Medical Center, in Lansing, Michigan, included everyone—nurses, mop boys, orderlies, secretaries. The head of the hospital spoke, stating that we might be the first person a visitor or patient had contact with, and they would form an opinion of the whole hospital based on us personally. They then held a scavenger hunt which we did in teams to find the X-ray department, Surgery, Central Supply, Pharmacy, the cafeteria, etc. We all left with a sense of importance (mission), a feeling of being part of a team, and from that day on, greeted visitors and patients with pleasure and confidence rather then considering them an interruption.

TIPS FOR IMPLEMENTATION:

One of the reasons this orientation process left such a positive impression on Dolores was because everyone started out their employment with the hospital as an equal, and thus, the organization instilled the idea that *everyone* is an important part of the team. The scavenger hunt was a team-building exercise that was both practical and fun and could be used in any organization's orientation!

Share and Learn from "Mis-Takes"

THE IDEA:

Most of us think of a "mistake" as "bad" or a "failure." However, because we are all human beings, there WILL be mistakes in our organizations. The question becomes not, "Will there be any mistakes?" but rather, "When we make a mistake, how will we handle it?" I ask people in my training sessions to hyphenate the word "mistake" and to think of it as a "MIS-TAKE." Doesn't that have a different feeling? I think of the movies where it may take hundreds of "takes" to get a final print. Therefore, a "MIS-TAKE" is not bad or a failure but rather just one thing that didn't work.

Most of us want to hide our mistakes; however, if you view them as "MIS-TAKES," then everyone can be comfortable to share theirs and all can learn from them.

THE IDEA IN ACTION:

An employee tells about how they handle "MIS-TAKES" in their office. The cashier who accumulates the most "voids" on a particular day gets a crown and the title of "Void King or Queen for the Day." They have chosen to have fun with what naturally will happen in their very stressful jobs.

One of the principals in an organization devoted to bringing more fun to the workplace shared in a conference presentation "awards" given internally in organizations for goofs. One example was a government organization which gives a "Brass Helmet" award when an employee makes a mis-take. This adds a spirit of fun and provides a way to talk about a difficult situation.

I even suggest to organizations that they have a "MIS-TAKE" of the week and have fun with whoever has made the biggest one. Not only does this create a wonderful sharing and learning atmosphere, but it also gives employees permission to admit their mis-takes and to fix them rather then pretending they didn't happen until an angry customer lets someone know. In fact, a "Mis-take," if fixed quickly and in a creative way, can become a wonderful opportunity to create a delighted customer and a more valuable employee!

TIPS FOR IMPLEMENTATION:

It may be difficult for some managers to lighten up enough to reframe a negative into a positive in this way; however, I have found that in organizations where employees are allowed to make mis-takes and are encouraged to share them, ultimately the number of mis-takes decreases because they are functioning in an atmosphere of support rather than fear. We live in the "Age of Empowerment," and while many informed managers are giving their employees *permission* to be empowered, many of them are not giving them *protection* when they make a Mis-take. If you give your employees both permission *and* protection, you will have employees who feel respected and valued, and that will translate to your bottom line.

Create a T-Shirt to Represent Your Organization's Values

THE IDEA:

One of the ideas I suggest in my booklet "49 Creative Ways to Get Your Ideas and Values Across" is to have a contest with your employees:

> *If my company or department were a T-shirt, this is what it would say..."*

Give them all the materials to actually design and create the shirt and then share their creations with the whole group.

THE IDEA IN ACTION:

Philippi-Hagenbuch, Inc., a company that makes accessories for off-highway mining equipment, recently did this activity with their whole company and voted on the best designs and slogans.

Another variation of this idea is one that Barry Berman, a trainer with Science Applications International Corporation, shared with me. He gives each person on a work team a blank chevron divided into 5 parts and asks them to each create their own personal "Coat of Arms," representing their diversity, their values, their uniqueness, and their purpose. These are the directions:

Space 1—Draw something that characterizes a peak performance in your life

Space 2—Sketch something about you that very few people know.

Space 3—Draw a symbol of how you like to spend your time.

Space 4—Fill in something that you are good at.

Space 5—Write or draw something that epitomizes your personal motto.

Other adaptations may include: Draw something that you love; draw what you most value in your life; write three characteristics that you want others to recognize in you; list three things you like about yourself; list three things you are working on in your life; write the name of one person or character, living or dead, with whom you'd like to spend an hour; draw a favorite childhood memory; draw your most embarrassing moment; draw the best present you have ever received; sketch an animal that represents you; write or draw one person, living or dead, who has been a hero for you; write what you would like as your epitaph.

TIPS FOR IMPLEMENTATION:

Have fun with this idea. If you do T-shirts, have all sorts of creative materials available—yarn, paints, flowers, buttons, glitter, string, different fabrics and prints, felt, feathers, snaps, hooks, and perhaps even appliqués. You can also do the exercise by making bumper stickers. You will be amazed at the dormant creativity in your co-workers!

Create a Mural

THE IDEA:

Create a mural depicting your organization's values, vision, or history. Be creative in finding a way for all employees to somehow be involved.

> **The person who succeeds is not the one who holds back, fearing failure, nor the one who never fails... but rather the one who moves on in spite of failure.**
>
> **CHARLES SWINDOLL**

THE IDEA IN ACTION:

Two years ago Saint Francis Medical Center in Peoria, Illinois, developed a vision of where they wanted to be by the year 1996. An artist created a montage mural for them depicting pictures symbolic of the new vision such as the Sisters, a helicopter, and bricks and mortar.

> **If a man is called to be a streetsweeper, he should sweep streets even as Michelangelo painted, or Beethoven composed music, or Shakespeare wrote poetry. He should sweep streets so well that all the hosts of heaven and earth will pause to say, here lived a great streetsweeper who did his job well.**
>
> **MARTIN LUTHER KING, JR.**

The 10½ by 7 foot mural was then made into a grid of 4400 one inch squares, each representing a person who contributes to the hospital's mission—the employees, the physicians, the Sisters, retirees, and the volunteers. Over two to three weeks the mural "traveled" to various offsite locations as well as the central facility, and each square was assigned ahead of time to one of the contributors who was asked to hand paint their own square. When people came in to paint their square, they were each given a T-shirt that said "SHARE THE VISION" on the back and the logo and "Saint Francis Medical Center" on the front as a lasting symbol of their participation in the project and the vision.

The final square was left for Sister M. Canisia, OSF, the Administrator of the hospital. When everyone had finished painting their squares, the mural was taken outside, and all available employees, physicians, and volunteers were asked to wear their T-shirts and attend the symbolic painting of the last square. The mural is hung in a high-traffic public hallway with a framed explanation of both the purpose and the process as a lasting reminder of their vision and "reason for being."

TIPS FOR IMPLEMENTATION:

I applaud the PR and Marketing departments of Saint Francis for their inclusion in a most personal way of ALL the people who contribute to their organization's everyday functioning. As you think of ways you can apply this idea in your own organization, keep in mind the beautiful spirit of community and purpose a project like this can create when *everyone* is invited to participate.

Our Lady of the Lake Regional Medical Center created a quilt for Hospital Week in their organization. Each department was asked to submit a quilt square to contribute to the whole that was then displayed for the first time to celebrate that week. Although departmental participation is not as powerful as individual participation, there is still pride involved in being a part of a project "of the whole."

Create Customer Gifts that Express the Organization's Values

THE IDEA:

It reinforces in a powerful way the company's values when they are incorporated into a meaningful gift, especially when employees have had a part in creating that gift.

THE IDEA IN ACTION:

 When I visited BI Performance Services, a Minneapolis-based company that helps organizations impact change through performance improvement, I was deeply touched by the beautifully framed

A star to guide us,
And a Child to lead the way.
A star,
And a Child.

There are no limits when we reach for the stars. Season's Greetings.

posters that lined the walls and hallways of the main building. Most of them were of people of all nationalities, ages, and backgrounds with animals or children. When I inquired about them, I learned that these are the Christmas cards that BI sends to its customers every year. They are created by BI artists and center around the themes of LOVE and RELATIONSHIPS, which are the central values held most dear by this family-owned company. These are some of the messages on the poster cards:

> *A great shared moment becomes a treasured memory.*
>
> *There's a light in the eyes of a child*
> *Irrepressible and joyful, innocent and honest,*
> *That dances and dazzles, and shines as a beacon*
> *Toward the greatest truth of all:* **IN LOVE IS OUR EVERLASTING STRENGTH**
>
> *Remember this holiday season to share the love you've learned to feel.*

Each one is signed, "The BI Family." They are a full poster size, and I am sure that their employees and customers have had them framed, just as I have, as symbols of the need for more love in our world.

 Mosby-Year Book, Inc., a publishing company in St. Louis, Missouri, this year beautifully reprinted a book that the founder of their company, Dr. Charles Virgil Mosby, wrote in 1917 called *Making the Grade*. This edition was reprinted as a gift for customers and employees "in recognition of Dr. Mosby who established The C.V. Mosby Company in 1906 with a dream of service to the healing arts. Dr. Mosby established and passed on to each succeeding generation the standards of excellence that we, as publishers, hold high today." What a very special way to commemorate a founder and share a vision!

TIPS FOR IMPLEMENTATION:

Involve your employees in thinking of creative ways to incorporate your organizational vision and values into gifts that can be both thought-provoking and lasting. These become a constant reminder of a company with a spirited workplace!

> In a churchyard in England this epitaph may be seen on a grave marker: *To Thomas Cobb who mended shoes in this village to the glory of God.*

Initiate a Program to "Celebrate the Mission"

THE IDEA:

In all organizations, the mission can become stale or even removed from the employees' daily work life. Creating a workshop or program to help employees recommit to the mission can work wonders to regenerate the spirit in a workplace.

THE IDEA IN ACTION:

The 2900 employees of Our Lady of the Lake Regional Medical Center, an 825-bed facility in Baton Rouge, Louisiana, felt the diminishing physical presence of their sponsor, the Franciscan Missionaries of Our Lady, so the Mission Effectiveness Committee commissioned a task force to develop a method for making the mission of the sisters come alive to the facility and all its employees. This commission resulted in a hospital-wide program to bring Christian values into focus and to put the spirit of the mission into daily practice.

> To love what you do and feel that it matters—how could anything be more fun?
>
> KATHERINE GRAHAM

The goals of the one-day workshop "Celebrate the Mission" are:

- To articulate the central values of Our Lady of the Lake Regional Medical Center to all employees
- To promote the Franciscan Missionary of Our Lady's mission of a healthcare ministry:

> **Our Lady of the Lake Regional Medical Center, as a Catholic health care facility, is committed to meeting the health needs of the people of God with compassion, understanding, respect, and dignity. The Medical Center is further dedicated to providing the highest quality health care in a prudent and efficient manner, in accordance with the philosophy of the Franciscan Missionaries of Our Lady.**

- To acknowledge and celebrate the creation of a vision by the sisters and the staff
- To allow a deep integration of the mission into daily work decisions.

This is the true joy in life, the being used for a purpose recognized by yourself as a mighty one; the being a force of nature instead of a feverish, selfish little clod of ailments and grievances complaining that the world will not devote itself to making you happy.

GEORGE BERNARD SHAW

To ensure that all of Our Lady of the Lake's 2900 employees experience "Celebrate the Mission," the program is offered twice a month but is limited to groups of no larger than 35 persons. Many employees, sisters, board members, and administrators facilitate "Celebrate the Mission" sessions.

The workshop focuses on a comparison of individual values, hospital values, and the values of the Franciscan Missionaries of Our Lady with employees coming to the realization that although we come from many races, religion, and socioeconomic backgrounds, we all have one thing in common—our core values.

Karen Profita says, "Celebrate the Mission has reduced turnover, improved morale, and even encouraged several employees to get their GED."

TIPS FOR IMPLEMENTATION:

One of the most important reasons why this program has been so successful is that it was developed and is presented by *employees for employees*. It is also designed around input from all levels of the organization and fosters communication from the bottom up and the top down. Another task force has been established to identify "Experience the Mission"—the next phase of the process to keep the values alive. The whole process can make a great difference not only in your organization's spirit but in the sense of spirit and purpose of each individual who participates. Many will go from being "slot fillers" to being truly committed to a mission larger than themselves.

Does your organization have an employee group charged with keeping the mission alive? Even creating a Mission Effectiveness Committee like Our Lady of the Lake can be a positive start. I think every organization should create a position for a Manager of Creativity, Vision, and Values!

Notes

1. Garfield, Charles. 1986. *Peak Performers*. New York, NY: William Morrow & Company, Inc.

2. Greene, Bob. 1992. "A choice lies behind each door." *Chicago Tribune*, Tempo, 25 August, p. 1.

Personal Action Ideas

Write your ideas here!

"Harvey? Harv Farnsworth? How the Heck are you? Say, I see you've finally lost that weight."

CHAPTER VIII

E = EMPATHY

It's a mistake to think we listen only with our ears. It's much more important to listen with the mind, the eyes, the body, and the heart. Unless you truly want to understand the other person, you'll never be able to listen.

MARK HERNDON

"Listening to Others with Your Heart as Well as Your Head"

Empathy, to me, means to really try to put yourself in the other person's place, to listen not just with your intellect but also with your heart to those unexpressed feelings of pain, lack of self-confidence, fear, unworthiness, and doubt. Stephen Covey in his book *The Seven Habits of Highly Successful People* says, "Seek first to understand and then to be understood."

David Noer, a vice president for the Center for Creative Leadership, a non-profit research and education institute in Greensboro, North Carolina, says that employees need to choose to let go of the anger and cynicism that has built up over the last 15 years, and executives need to choose to acknowledge their pain.[1]

The Chinese characters which make up the verb "to listen" tell us something significant about this skill.

Ear

You

Eyes

Undivided Attention

Heart

My brother, who is a consultant in Singapore, sent me the Chinese symbol for the verb "to listen."

On the left hand side, the ear is represented—listening with our head; however, on the right side we see listening from our own personhood, with our eyes for body language, with our undivided attention, and the cornerstone is listening with our hearts. Are you and the leaders in your organization listening with your hearts?

The Chinese symbol for "people" makes an interesting statement, for one stroke is upheld by the other. So it is in our organizations. We need to support each other as we journey through this time of unprecedented change and confusion. As this character shows, each stroke is strengthened by the action of the other. But the removal of either will cause both to fall.

Empathy encompasses a celebration of diversity, valuing, and rejoicing in our differences. Valuing differences in the workplace is a

key ingredient in employee morale. When employees feel that their work and their perspectives are recognized and appreciated, their morale is high. One of the most beautiful stories of diversity and valuing differences I have ever found is the children's book *Stellaluna* by Janell Cannon (1993). It is the story of a baby bat whose mother drops it, and it falls into a robin's nest where it lives for a long time. Stellaluna tries and tries to be like the robins until one day she meets a bunch of bats and finds her mother again. What a wonderful relief to finally be able to sleep upside down! At the end of the book after Stellaluna saves the little robins when they try to fly with her in the dark, she is back in the young robins' nest, and this is their conversation:

> "We're safe," said Stellaluna. Then she sighed, "I wish you could see in the dark, too."
>
> "We wish you could land on your feet," Flitter replied. Pip and Flap nodded.
>
> They perched in silence for a long time.
>
> "How can we be so different and feel so much alike?" mused Flitter.
>
> "And how can we feel so different and be so much alike?" wondered Pip.
>
> "I think this is quite a mystery," Flap chirped.
>
> "I agree, " said Stellaluna. "But we're friends. And that's a fact."[2]

In your place of work are you rejoicing in your differences, acknowledging others' pain, and finding new ways to care about each individual?

Social Responsibility: Care about the World Outside Your Lobby

It gives you a feeling of being someone. It feels as though someone cares. And that, that's uplifting, spiritual.

JOHN R.S. LEWIS, A HOMELESS PERSON
Speaking about the Dignity Diner, a meal program sponsored by Holy Covenant United Methodist Church

THE IDEA:

Support efforts in your community to make life better for all, particularly if there is a crisis of some kind. This is also a wonderful way for an organization or work team to better learn to work together and to demonstrate its values.

THE IDEA IN ACTION:

During the St. Louis floods, Spectrum Healthcare Services instituted a "Buy a Casual Day" program. They asked employees to contribute $1 for every day that they'd like to dress casually. The money was then donated to the Red Cross, which in turn helped the flood victims. In this example, according to Patricia Keeley, the Manager of Human Resource Development, the victims AND the employees benefited. They even suggested that employees might write a check for $365 and make it a casual day year-round!

One of the telephone centers of APAC Teleservices became concerned about the community shelters needing food in the summertime. Around Thanksgiving, Christmas, and Easter, they felt people were more aware of the needs and remembered to contribute canned goods, but no one thought about the shelters in the summer. To encourage employees to remember, they decided that if an employee brought in two cans of food, they could wear jeans and sneakers to work that day. They helped others AND had fun!

Blanchard Training and Development has a fund called "BTD for Others." Employees collect money to adopt needy families, and

Ken and Margie Blanchard, the owners of the company, match that amount. Then they all work together to share their blessings by helping the families in need.

 The Tuesday, October 3, edition of *The Wall Street Journal* tells this story:

> Jerry Gregoire, head of information technology for PepsiCo, Inc., in Purchase, New York, grew tired of the usual programs that companies use to foster staff bonding. So last week he and his staff of more than 350 renovated the Children's Village for troubled boys in Dobbs Ferry, New York, painting the houses and rebuilding basketball courts and playgrounds.[3]

What a very special way to share in a purpose greater than just having a social time together!

 Performance Systems Corporation in Dallas, Texas, implemented a wonderful contribution to their community and world called "Project PSC." It was a profitable year for the company and consequently, they "shared the wealth" in a very unique manner. During the holiday season, each employee was given $1000 to contribute to the charity of their choice. PSC was awarded the 1993 Outstanding Volunteer of the Year Award by the City of Dallas for their generosity. It is also deeply fitting for this company because the principals are the authors of the book *Walk the Talk!* Not only did they share their blessings as an organization, but they also allowed each employee to have a special, personal part in that sharing.

 The Gibbs family, owners of Gibbs Country House, a restaurant in Ludington, Michigan, have sponsored a special program they call "Not By Bread Alone" for many years. This interdenominational inspirational luncheon series is based on the scripture, "Man does not live on bread alone but on every word that comes from the mouth of God." It is an opportunity on the fourth Thursday of every month for both men and women to gather and hear someone's story of God's provision and presence in his or her life. The family furnishes the lunch and the speakers, and a freewill offering is taken to defray the cost of the lunch. They average from 30 to 70 guests, and employees are also invited to attend. What a very special way to share their values and to give back to their community!

An employee of a state department of social services shared with me a wonderful story of how her office worked together to create a special experience for one of their clients. He is a Vietnam veteran who lives in the woods and supports himself by collecting pop cans along the sides of the road. Everyone in the state office had grown fond of him as he came in on a regular basis and decided that they wanted to do something for him for Christmas last year, since he seems to have no other family. Not wanting to embarrass him, they began to save all their pop cans at home, and the week before Christmas, they all brought them in and found they had collected several huge garbage bags of cans. When he came into the office that week, one of the employees drove out to his camp while he was still in the office and would not know who was responsible, and left all the sacks of cans, several plates of homemade goodies that co-workers had made, and an anonymous note reading, "Merry Christmas." Their creative caring certainly made a difference, both to the spirit in their office and to a hurting individual.

TIPS FOR IMPLEMENTATION:

You may reach out to your community as a work team, as an organization, or as an individual who represents his or her place of work. For example, there are literally thousands of organizations who could use volunteer help. Habitat for Humanity builds houses for the homeless, and some corporations are sending management teams to work on Habitat projects to learn how to REALLY work together. Other work groups commit to helping clean up along the highway or plant flowers in the downtown area. Research those nonprofit organizations in your area and particularly remember those that help the most needy, our children. The "Buy a Casual Day" idea could be used for just about any fundraising activity. However, it is most significant if there is a real mission or purpose involved such as a natural catastrophe, helping a co-worker who has had an illness or a fire, or supporting a cause in the local community, and the more actively involved employees are, the more it will rekindle the spirit in your workplace.

Let Employees Experience Being Guests

THE IDEA:

One of the best ways to create a new spirit of caring and concern in the workplace is to allow employees the opportunity to experience service as a customer.

THE IDEA IN ACTION:

At the Holiday Inn South in Lansing, Michigan, all the front desk employees and bellmen were given the opportunity to be guests in the hotel for a day. They stayed in Preferred Quarters, ate in the restaurant, went to the pool, ordered room service, and called for extra items as a guest—extra pillows, toothpaste, and iron and board.

One of the bellmen told me that not only was it "really fun," but that it helped him understand more about what the guests go through and how it feels, and it made him really proud to be a part of their organization.

TIPS FOR IMPLEMENTATION:

Think of creative ways you can allow your employees on company time to experience being a customer. The information you will gain will be invaluable, and you will have created some very loyal employees!

Sponsor Community Seminars

THE IDEA:

One way to give back to your community and to create a feeling of understanding and goodwill for your organization is to sponsor community seminars and programs, regardless of whether they have anything to do with your business or industry.

Hills Bank & Trust Company

THE IDEA IN ACTION:

Hills Bank and Trust Company in Iowa City, Iowa, does a great deal to make a difference in the community. They have held community conferences on "Making Schools Fit Children," "Seeking the American Dream—Intercultural Understanding," and a seminar on the importance of human relations in the workplace called "Positive Leadership Works." It focused on the value of creating enthusiasm, being kind and considerate, and fostering positive attitudes to make the workplace more enjoyable and rewarding.

They also co-sponsor a "Community Reading Month." They have distributed over 400 t-shirts to people in the community that say:

Just **R***ecommend it*
E*xperience it*
A*chieve it*
D*ream it*

They also do a special summer reading project in Coralville, Iowa. This summer they had about 1200 kids sign up for the Coralville Reading Project, and the entire town only has about 6000! They sponsor a Chapter One reading program in the fall and high school leadership conferences to recognize over 250 high school students from eastern Iowa.

One of the bank managers said, "We have no official corporate philosophy or motto regarding these projects. In trying to figure out why Hills Bank and Trust Company has grown to become the largest bank in the community, our best guess is that we do meaningful community projects which has created an identity for Hills Bank and has allowed our staff to develop personal relationships with people in the community."

A Supermarket Branch of a large bank in Idaho is sponsoring a weekly "Bank Day" savings program at a local elementary school. A personal retail banker visited each class in grades 1–6 and presented a program on savings accounts. Students were then encouraged to open up a minor savings account. Each week, two associates from the branch office visit the school to open up new savings accounts and to help existing account holders with their accounts. What a wonderful service to help educate the next generation on the importance of "saving for the future!"

TIPS FOR IMPLEMENTATION:

No matter what the size of your organization, you can provide opportunities to educate and encourage people in your community. Get employees involved—they will feel good about sharing with others, and they will experience the positive affirmation the community will give both them and your organization. For example, some employees of city banks are offering free seminars at night in inner city neighborhoods for lower income and older people who need basic financial advice.

Make a Caring Phone Call

THE IDEA:

At least once a week call someone, either an internal or external customer, just to let them know that you are thinking about them. If you can't reach them personally, leave a caring voice mail message. I can vouch for how much that can brighten someone's day!

THE IDEA IN ACTION:

R. Joan Stewart, Vice President of the Metro Decatur Chamber of Commerce, Decatur, Illinois, wrote me about a caring call she received:

> Several years ago, I entered Decatur Memorial Hospital as an outpatient. While there, I experienced the "lower GI series." No fun! The next day while recuperating at home, I received a call from an employee of DMH. When she identified herself, I thought, "Calling about the bill? About test results?" But, no! She said, "I know we put you through some rough tests yesterday, and I am calling to see how you feel."
>
> Wow! A little thing? Yes. Effective? Yes. For whatever her time in calling me cost DMH, the return on investment has been great. I tell the story every time Customer Relations comes up in meetings and in one-on-one conversations. The good PR DMH receives can't be bought for any amount of money, but a caring phone call did it!

A person in one of my programs told me about a Supermarket Branch in an Albertson's Grocery Store in Washington which went even beyond the caring phone call. After finding out that two of the branch's customers were in the hospital at the same time, the staff visited and delivered flowers to both individuals. One of these customers, who lives across the street from the branch, needed help getting his groceries home while he recuperated from his hospital stay. A personal retail banker volunteered twice to deliver groceries to the customer's house during his recovery period. Her extra special caring has truly helped regenerate the spirit in her workplace, and she has become a model for all of the bank!

TIPS FOR IMPLEMENTATION:

Come up with a personal strategy to make this caring phone call a habit. Perhaps pick a day of the week that you will make your call and then write "CC" on your calendar for that day each week, or have a weekly check list and don't leave your office on Friday until you have made at least one caring call.

Or make a caring call each day just before you go to lunch. Choose whatever will work for you to "whack" your thinking and make you really remember to do it. You will experience as much joy as the person you call!

> **Empathy is your pain in my heart.**
>
> ANONYMOUS

Be an Encourager

THE IDEA:

Use creative ways to support and encourage others in their own growth and development.

THE IDEA IN ACTION:

Diane Carden, the owner of Daystar Productions in Lutz, Florida, at the end of a facilitator training session gives each of the participants "Facilitator Survival Kits." They include party blowers to show that "they are responsible for spreading contagious enthusiasm"; Chuckles candy to "remember the humor in mis-takes"; a blank 'thank you' note to encourage them to "model giving affirmation and appreciation"; a key chain with a metal tool on it to "remember the Tools of good communication"; Halls cough drops and bandaids for "emergencies"; and a package of alka seltzer for

> **The heart understands what the mind can never comprehend.**
>
> CHARLIE HATCH

"Listen, the reason you didn't get the last job wasn't because you're a Jackass, it's because you don't know word processing."

"when it is all over!" She also gives each participant a package of seeds to take home with them. She says, "No matter how much experience we have, we can always give ourselves room to grow." This has become her personal signature as a trainer and encourages participants to stretch and be the best they can be!

 Og Mandino says in a promotional brochure:

> *Realize what a unique and shining*
> *star you are.*
> *No one who came before you,*
> *No one that lives today, and*

*No one that comes tomorrow
Can walk, talk, move, and think like you.*

One organization I worked with used this thought for a huge bulletin board in their lobby. They then asked each employee to sign his or her name on a big gold star, and they posted them all over the board. The board was titled, "Our Company Stars." What a wonderful way to make everyone feel special!

Judy Constantino, a senior training consultant for Kaset International, told me about how she encourages others. She makes them "Sunshine Baskets" that are filled with seven or more individually wrapped gifts or cards with the instructions to open one each day and know that someone is thinking of you. She includes such things as packets of bubble bath, special teas, little booklets, small boxes of candy, tiny stuffed animals, lovely quotations, and other small remembrances.

Maria Marino, the president of Swinging on a Cloud in London, Ontario, Canada sends anonymous gifts to fellow employees during tough times—uplifting poems, guardian angel pins, and even pretty-smelling hand cream.

TIPS FOR IMPLEMENTATION:

Think of special ways you can encourage others and then DO IT! We all have emotional bank accounts, and each day we get deposits and withdrawals. When you notice a co-worker whose account is nearly overdrawn, make a deposit. When you do, you will receive a deposit in your account, too!

Trade Jobs with Someone in the Organization

THE IDEA:

One of the best ways to promote understanding, empathy, and teamwork throughout an organization is provide a way for employees to trade jobs with someone else in the organization for a short period of time. When I was working with the state of Minnesota doing customer service training several years ago, we asked all state employees what they would like as a reward for giving good customer service. The number one thing they requested was "to trade jobs with someone else in the state for a half day." They wanted to feel more a part of a team.

> **The capacity to care is the thing which gives life its deepest meaning and significance.**
>
> **PABLO CASALS**

THE IDEA IN ACTION:

At Saint Francis Medical Center in Peoria, Illinois, High Performance Team #7 developed a program called "Walk In My Shoes" to promote partnerships between and among their many employees. For example, if you work on a nursing unit and wonder how a laboratory worker fits into the care you provide patients, you can spend an hour or two with a person in the lab. Or if you are in health information services and want to understand the workings of surgery, you may take a couple of hours and visit the surgery unit:

> **In each human heart are a tiger, a pig, an ass, and a nightingale . . . Diversity of character is due to their unequal activity.**
>
> **AMBROSE BIERCE**

How does it work? Just get together with your supervisor and tell him or her which area you would like to visit. After some paperwork is completed and specific time/date arrangements are made, you'll be ready to walk in the shoes of another.

TIPS FOR IMPLEMENTATION:

One of the three things all employees want is a "feeling of being in on things," so this program will accomplish many objectives.

Hire Some "Moms"

THE IDEA:

Who knows better how to nurture than Moms? And who do most of us think of when we're really down and need some tender loving care? Organizations who truly care about their employees can make "nurturing" a part of someone's *real* job!

THE IDEA IN ACTION:

At Evolving Systems, Inc., a computer software company in Englewood, Colorado, they have five and a half full-time "Moms" and one full-time "Dad," one for every 80–90 employees. Their whole job consists in giving personal attention to the employees, and they report directly to the president of the company, Harry Fair, the founder of the Moms. Nita Cronin, whose title is "Lead Mom," shared with me a little about their job, which is to create a unique, happy, friendly environment and to add the comforts of home to the workplace.

One of their primary jobs, besides knowing each employee by name and a little bit about them and their families, is to keep all 18 kitchens (every wing in each building has two kitchens) stocked just as they would be at home—with dishes, silver, napkins, paper towels, fruit baskets, daily fresh fruit juices, coffee, tea, and condiments. There are also free soda and beverage dispensing machines available.

The Moms provide daily snacks, both morning and afternoon, of such things as cheese and crackers, fruit plates, carrot and celery sticks, and breakfast bars that they put out in the kitchens. They have a budget to stock the kitchens, so there is no charge to the employees for any of this. Nita said, "If employees are working and they are hungry, they break their mindset and lose productivity if they have to go out to a convenience store, so we make it possible for them to go to the kitchen and get a small snack at any time of the day or night."

The Moms also select two restaurants a day, and they order in meals for the employees if they wish. Each employee has an account with them, so the lunch can be charged, which makes it extremely convenient. Nita says that if an employee isn't feeling well or has an injury, they deliver the lunches right to their desks! They provide birthday cakes at company meetings and even give employees little birthday gifts such as stress toys and balloons. They plan parties, open houses, and anniversaries and provide all sorts of valuable information and advice to their fellow employees.

> **Why is it that people always need love and understanding the most at a time when they probably deserve it the least?**
>
> Lou Holtz

The Moms want their office to be a fun place to be so that employees will "come to see Mom!" They stock candy, medications, pantyhose, eye drops, eye glass repair kits, dental floss, toothbrushes and paste, and even shoelaces—all provided by the company. "The Mom's job is to come in with a smile and to be morale boosters," says Nita. "We spend a good part of our day 'out and about', watering plants, saying 'hi' to employees, inquiring about their families and hobbies, and finding out what is going on with them. When someone has a deadline, we try to drop off special treats to encourage them and thank them for their hard work, or if they aren't feeling well, we check to see how they're doing and what they might need. We even mail things for employees when they are too busy."

The company looks for warm, caring, upbeat people to be their Moms, and they are interviewed by the president himself. The philosophy of the company is, "If you can provide a good working environment, you can create better products." And that is exactly what the Moms are there to do!

> **The more high technology around us, the more the need for the human touch.**
>
> John Naisbitt
> *Megatrends*

TIPS FOR IMPLEMENTATION:
Isn't this a wonderful idea to help regenerate spirit in any workplace? Obviously, the benefits must far outweigh the costs at Evolving Systems, Inc. Happy employees ARE more productive employees without a doubt, and all of us could use a little more nurturing! Couldn't your organization use a "Mom"?

Share Vacation Time

THE IDEA:

One very special way to create a wonderful spirit of empathy and caring in your organization is to have a policy that employees can share their vacation time with others. This idea was first suggested by employees and then adopted by management.

THE IDEA IN ACTION:

Catherine Angeli, the manager of the Gogebic and Iron County offices of the Michigan Department of Social Services, told me about a decision that was mutually reached between Labor Relations and their Central Office during a recent heartrending incident in their office. An employee's seven-year-old son was discovered to be terminally ill with cancer, and the employee wanted to be able to stay home with him during his last days. However, she had very little vacation time left. When a number of her co-workers volunteered to give her some of their leave time, it was decided that other DSS employees could donate up to 240 total hours of their time to share with the mother of the little boy. Employees from the Marquette, Houghton, and Gogebic offices all volunteered days of their own vacation time, and even when the maximum number of hours had been donated, calls were still coming in. There have been other cases throughout the state of Michigan of employees donating their vacation time to co-workers in crisis. What a very special way to show their empathy and care!

One of the stories in the "Random Acts of Kindness" column in the Saint Francis Medical Center "Carrillon" newsletter in Peoria, Illinois, mentions employees sharing vacation time:

> *Mary Vancil, ICU, wants to thank her co-workers who donated vacation time to her when her husband suffered a heart attack and required surgery.*

TIPS FOR IMPLEMENTATION:

I think it helps for an organization have a written policy that gives employees *permission* to be able to donate their vacation time. In one case, an employee wanted to donate time to a co-worker in distress, but because she was a union member and the other person was not, the details could not be worked out to make that happen. When crises occur, there is no time for bureaucracy and Red Tape!

Go Out of Your Way to Welcome New Employees

THE IDEA:

Think of fun, creative ways to make new employees feel welcome. If they begin work in an atmosphere of caring, they will be much more likely to continue adding to that atmosphere.

THE IDEA IN ACTION:

One organization with whom I've worked arranges lunch with the president of the company for every new employee during his/her first week. Another has created a special company shirt that new employees are asked to wear for the first month they are on the job. (Yes, they give them two for laundry purposes!) Whenever anyone sees a person with the shirt on, they make it a point to introduce themselves and do something special for that person. One employee told me that she was so specially treated that she NEVER wants to work anywhere else!

Maria Marino, the President of Swinging on a Cloud in London, Ontario, Canada creates welcome kits for new staff complete with a welcome card signed by each employee, a fun name tag, a map, and other goodies to make them feel special.

TIPS FOR IMPLEMENTATION:

Remember what it felt like when you were new. What can you do to help someone else have a better experience than you did? It is easiest to show empathy when you've "been there!"

Celebrate Random Acts of Kindness

THE IDEA:

What wisdom can you find that is greater than kindness?

JOHN JACQUES ROUSSEAU

Create a vehicle to celebrate on a regular basis random acts of kindness, both internally and externally.

THE IDEA IN ACTION:

Kindness is more important than wisdom, and the recognition of this is the beginning of wisdom.

THEODORE ISAAC RUBIN

Saint Francis Medical Center in Peoria, Illinois, has a column in its newsletter "Carillon" that is called "Random Acts of Kindness." It reads, "Show your wisdom by showing your kindness to people you encounter at work and wherever you may go. It's also kind to acknowledge others for their kind deeds. You can report acts of kindness by calling the Kindness Hotline at 655-4555."

> **The worst sin towards our fellow creatures is note to hate them, but to be indifferent to them; that's the essence of inhumanity.**
>
> **GEORGE BERNARD SHAW**

Here are some of the acts of kindness reported:

Michelle Asple from Cardiovascular Intensive Care extends a thank-you to Kathy from the Mother-Baby Care Unit for her recent act of kindness. When Michelle's truck wouldn't start after she got off work late one night around 11:30 p.m., Kathy insisted on staying with her in the parking lot until a security officer arrived to jump-start the vehicle. Kathy also offered to take Michelle home if the truck still wouldn't start or to follow her home to make sure she didn't have more car trouble.

Ronda Guengerich, RN from 5100, wants to share a patient-to-patient act of kindness she witnessed. A male patient on the unit observed that a young female patient seen in the hallway looked depressed. He was concerned about his fellow patient and made some inquiries about her. He found out that she had been hospitalized for quite a while and that Ronda had been trying to get a video game system to her to use to cheer her up and help pass the time. The concerned patient called his fiancee and asked her to purchase a Sega Genesis and games as a gift for the patient.

While on his way to Saint Francis to make a delivery, Ted Hacker, a courier from the East Peoria Outpatient Center, stopped to help two women change a flat tire.

Jean Kolvoord, Mary Leitner, Darlene Lohnes, Annette NcNicol, Nancy Thomas, and Nancy Weaver from Patient Care Administration report that a recent departmental move would have taken a lot longer had it not been for the kind assistance of Wayne Kolvoord. Wayne, Jean's husband, volunteered his time on a vacation day to move and organize PCA's supply room.

TIPS FOR IMPLEMENTATION:

What a wonderful way to encourage employees to be more kind and to make everyone who reads the column feel uplifted!

Begin a "Kindness Campaign"

THE IDEA:

You can begin a focus on kindness in your department, building, organization, school, or even in your community. The beautiful little book *Random Acts of Kindness* has opened many people's eyes to the positive impact of small deeds. Encouraging and celebrating these deeds in a formal way is the focus of a "Kindness Campaign."

THE IDEA IN ACTION:

Rita Blitt, a painter/sculptor and the artist who created the drawings in this book, told me of a very special program which began in Kansas City with her words, "Kindness is Contagious . . . Catch it!"

Rita envisioned a kindness program for children, and she knew that her friend, SuEllen Fried, could organize it. Soon after that, SuEllen, also of Kansas City and founder of the STOP Violence Coalition, involved several children's classes in focus groups to talk about bullying and the cruelty of children to one another. To reduce the incidence of teasing, they came up with the idea of placing two jars in the classroom, one labeled "PUT DOWNS" and the other "PUT UPS." Tokens of some kind would be placed around the jars, and whenever someone received a put-down or a put-up, they would place a token in the jar. As imagined, the visual concept had a dramatic impact on the behavior of the children, and they became much kinder to one another.

Barbara Unell, editor and publisher of TWINS magazine and a Board member of the STOP Violence Coalition, took this idea to the guidance counselor at her children's school, and soon a pro-

Kindness is contagious.
CATCH IT!

Blitt 86-91

gram was born. Another idea called "Pass it On" was added. In this activity, when a teacher spotted a child performing a kind act, he/she placed a special eraser on the child's desk and then asked that child to become the observer of a kind act and pass the eraser on. Adults participate in this activity now by wearing a button that says, "Kindness is Contagious . . . Catch it!" and then pass it on to other people who perform acts of kindness. Legendary stories have evolved as these buttons have spread all over the country!

A partnership developed with a local TV station, KMBC-TV, which sends a letter out to every school district each fall asking the children to nominate the "Kindest Kansas Citians." Over 4000 nominations are returned each year, and three winners are selected and honored at a Kindness dinner. Students write touching stories about coaches, teachers, school custodians, bus drivers, and others who have touched their lives, and the evening is filled with tears of joy.

At the very first Kindness dinner, Rita Blitt was asked to create a small sculpture for each of the "Kindest Kansas Citians" and to present each of the children who read their winning letters a print using her art work and her words, "Kindness is Contagious . . . Catch it!" Instead of ordering a few prints to be made, however, Rita decided to order 2500! She has made it a personal campaign to send them all over the world, whenever and wherever she has heard of a kind person, hoping to plant seeds of kindness. They have been sent to nearly every state as well as 183 foreign nations.

The "Kindness is Contagious...Catch it!" activity program guide has now spread to 300 schools in the greater Kansas City area as well as 34 states and Ontario, Canada. Many, many folks have become involved in helping to bring more kindness and love to the lives of the residents of greater Kansas City as well as in other cities throughout North America. As the circle of good deeds grows, that kindness and love is spread throughout the world.

The program guide on Kindness lists "10 Ways You Can Help Spread an Epidemic of Kindness" that we can all apply in our everyday work lives:

1. Take time to listen.

3. Forgive someone who hurt you.

4. Apologize for something you've done wrong.

5. Do a favor for someone in need.

6. Give hugs.

7. Compromise. Don't start a fight.

8. Negotiate. Don't blame.

9. Empathize. Don't gossip.

10. Problem-solve. Don't tease or name-call.

TIPS FOR IMPLEMENTATION:

No matter where you work, you can begin a campaign of Kindness. What a very special way to add more caring and spirit to our world! In the words of Ivan Misic, the Ambassador to the UN from the Republic of Bosnia and Herzogovina, "The highest form of power is not the allocation of external resources, but the harnessing of internal ones. Let us harness the love of all the people of the world. Love, and love alone, can undo hatred." For information on the Kindness campaign, see the listing for the STOP Violence Coalition in the Resources section of the book.

Notes

1. Miller Rubin, Bonnie. 1995. "The Death of Ambition." *Chicago Tribune Magazine*, 22 January, p. 15.

2. Excerpt from *Stellaluna*, copyright 1993 by Janell Cannon, reprinted by permission of Harcourt Brace & Company.

3. Editors. 1995. "Teamwork." *Wall Street Journal*, 3 October.

Personal Action Ideas

Write your ideas here!

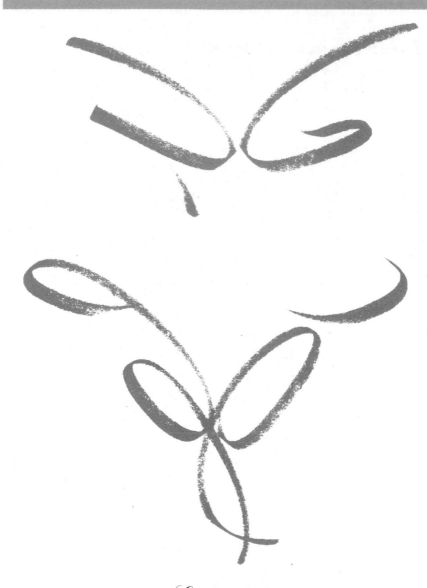

Enthusiasm

Years wrinkle the skin, but to give up enthusiasm wrinkles the soul.

Samuel Ullman

CHAPTER IX

E = Enthusiasm

If you're working in a company that is not ENTHUSIASTIC, energetic, creative, clever, curious, and just plain fun, you've got troubles, serious troubles.

TOM PETERS

"Celebrate Your Team with Joy!"

I personally believe that enthusiasm is the most important element of a spirited workplace. People will do things they don't really want to do if someone else inspires them with their enthusiasm. I found the following quotation from Francis Likert several years ago, and from it, I extracted my own personal motto, "SPREADING CONTAGIOUS ENTHUSIASM":

> If a high level of performance is to be achieved, it appears to be necessary for a supervisor to have high performance goals and a contagious enthusiasm as to the importance of these goals.

Haven't you ever learned things that you really didn't want to learn because the teacher was so enthusiastic about the subject? If

"Well, yes I do remember, "Have a nice day", but there doesn't seem to be much else on your resume."

managers are enthusiastic about the importance of the job their department or division is doing, then that enthusiasm spreads to each employee. However, contagious enthusiasm does NOT have to start at the top. Even one enthusiastic employee with a deep sense of mission and purpose can inspire those around to achieve their very best, so let enthusiasm begin with YOU!

Some of us are blessed to be able to do what we love. I would share my thoughts and learnings with groups even if I didn't get paid because I have such a deep sense of mission about helping all of us see the choices we have to make a difference. However, many people do not love their jobs; in fact, they may even feel trapped and abused.

The challenge is to find your own passion—what small thing about your job *can* you love? Perhaps it is the freedom to make your own choices or the people with whom you interact or working with figures or keeping those around you organized or writing copy or just seeing a result at the end of the day. If you can discover something that gives you a sense of purpose, then concentrate on that, and I believe you can find a new enthusiasm for your work.

As enthusiasm spreads throughout your workplace, you will see employees who are more committed to their jobs, who enjoy being at work, and who are having fun doing things they believe in.

Have Departmental or Team Skits

THE IDEA:

One special way to engender spirit and enthusiasm is to assign different groups in the organization to perform skits at company or departmental meetings.

THE IDEA IN ACTION:

Artex International, a company in Highland, IL, that specializes in quality table linens, held an all-company quality rally in June. As a part of the rally they asked various teams in the organization to perform skits that related to the three areas of their quality focus: Customer Satisfaction, Associate Involvement, and Process Improvement. The teams had been formed as a result of someone in the company submitting an OFI (Opportunity for Improvement), indicating a problem that needed to be solved. Teams that had worked on specific problems were chosen by the quality council to perform a skit related to their particular OFI.

Some of the wonderfully creative skits were "The Work Order Orderlies" (a problem with the submission process for work orders); "Unseamly" (sometimes napkins were sent out with a seam in the middle); "The Short Cutters"; "Customer Connections" (customers were having problems with returns); and "The Six Shooters"

The Clarion Hotel in Virginia Beach, Virginia, assigns one department each month to present a "Bad Service / Good Service" skit at their monthly pep rally.

TIPS FOR IMPLEMENTATION:

Get as many of your employees as possible involved in skits at different times, and make sure that they relate in some way to the values you hold in the organization. People love to create and to laugh—and the chance to be "on stage" brings out the delightful child in most of us. For those who are shy, there is always a need for props and sound people. Not only will your employees have fun, but you will begin collecting company legends as well as seeing talent you didn't know existed! ALWAYS have a camcorder available to capture these creations for posterity.

Offer Inspirational, Uplifting Training

THE IDEA:

One powerful way to motivate employees whose morale is low is to offer high-quality training that impacts their self-esteem and gets their creative juices going. They need to realize that even though many changes are going on around them, they still have CHOICES and can make a difference in every one-on-one interaction they have regardless of what their job is, what their bosses or co-workers are doing, or how many technological changes are occurring. THEY ARE IMPORTANT!

THE IDEA IN ACTION:

 I recently did a session I call "Send a C.A.R.E. Package—Regenerate the Spirit in your Organization" for three different groups. One was the Institute of Financial Education, an organization that serves financial institutions all over the country. Another was Bachrach

Clothing, a retail company with both stores and a large catalog division. The third was the Regency Square Shopping Mall in Richmond, Virginia, where I spoke to all the store employees. These are three of the letters I received attesting to the day-to-day, actionable difference the message of hope and caring made:

> If I may share a quick story with you . . . After your session, I realized that I needed to relate to my assistant on a more balanced level. I had accomplished the "business/skill" level without a problem but I didn't seem to be in balance with her at the "human/love" level. So, my goal now is to build on this theory and "expect a masterpiece." Thank you so much for regenerating the spirit in ME. I'm on a mission to share "contagious enthusiasm" with everyone!
>
> *Eileen Nepomuceno, Chapter President*
> *Honolulu, Hawaii*

> We had a large department meeting the Saturday after the workshop and we passed out buttons that say "I'M A MANAGER" to everyone. A lot of the phone counselors are putting their personal signatures on orders by keying-in "Have a nice day" on the paperwork included with the order or keying-in their name and extension in case the customer has a question, etc. We're also having a big banner made that says "WE MANAGE MOMENTS OF TRUTH!"
>
> The credit department is sending McDonald's gift certificates to store people calling in with problems with a note saying that we hoped we took care of things for them and to let us know if we can do anything else. So, as you can see, your workshop definitely fueled our creative juices!
>
> *Kathy Kuhlenbeck, Chief Financial Officer*
> *Bachrach Clothing, Decatur, Illinois*

> Barbara,
>
> I had the absolute worst day and had dealt with what seemed to be the worst people at the time. Very downhearted, I came to the seminar, and the last thing on my mind was worrying about my customer's needs—"What about me? Why should I be nice to everyone else?"

> Thank you for caring—you knocked my socks off and brought tears to my eyes twice and renewed my spirit. I'm walking away much better and happier than when I came in!
>
> *A store employee*
> *Regency Square Mall, Richmond, Virginia*

 Another card I received after a workshop contained this note:

> I could never put into words the impact our training session has already had in my life. I cried all the way home Wednesday night, feeling so cleansed of all the negative power in my life. I also turned down the wrong street and drove five miles before I realized I was going the wrong way, thinking about how I am going to put into practice the new behaviors I learned. Already my family sees the difference and I hope I can share that same difference with my customers and co-workers.

 Bill Athayde, former Executive Vice President at Industrial Marine Service, Inc., (IMS) in Norfolk, Virginia, tells of an employee who had been with them for years. She was offered a 25 percent wage increase to go to another company, but decided to stay with IMS even though they could only offer her a 6 percent raise. One of the main reasons she stayed was because they were going to offer some special training in continuous quality improvement and teamwork. On day two of the training, she was nearly in tears and told them she was "so happy she didn't take that other job." This was the first time she had been offered any training, and for the very first time employees were told that their opinions mattered. This same woman just recently told Bill, "Boss, we need a Pep Rally!"

TIPS FOR IMPLEMENTATION:

I have found that many employees have never had an opportunity to hear a motivational speaker. Often those experiences are "reserved" for upper level management and salespeople. Even if you can't afford to bring a real live speaker for the whole company, have a brown bag lunch and watch an inspirational videotape. Find one with inspiration, humor, and actionable ideas, and you will be making an invaluable investment that will result in both happier employees AND happier customers!

Create an Attitude Support Team

THE IDEA:

Create a team of people chosen from each department to be the Cheerleaders/ Motivators/ Morale Builders/ Encouragers throughout your organization.

THE IDEA IN ACTION:

Cottrell, Ltd., a medical/dental protection manufacturer in Englewood, Colorado, asked each functional group to select one person to be their Attitude Champion and to serve on a company-wide Attitude Advisory Board.

Using input from each department, the committee created its **Purpose Statement:**

> *Our commitment is to promote ongoing interactive communication, encourage teamwork, and inspire positive morale throughout* our world. We *will be proactive in initiating activities, seeking solutions, and making recommendations in support of our company and each other.*

At each company meeting, they report their accomplishments such as the creation of a calendar, better communication with management, their purpose statement, a potluck, a casual day, and efforts towards creating new award criteria. They have even handed out a copy of their purpose statement to everyone in the company.

TIPS FOR IMPLEMENTATION:

This idea could be started at any level of the organization or even within a team itself. These champions can be the catalyst to regenerate the spirit in their workplaces.

Encourage Social Events and Celebrations

> Find something that you love to do and you'll never have to work a day in your life!
>
> **HARVEY MACKAY**

THE IDEA:

Celebrate real holidays, special successes, and any other occasions. A workplace filled with a celebratory spirit will bring joy to all, both employees and customers!

THE IDEA IN ACTION:

Spectrum Healthcare Services in St. Louis, Missouri, celebrates just about every holiday in a special way. It usually involves placing a small token on the employee's desk prior to them arriving at work. For example:

- A "You Are Loved" pin on Valentine's Day
- Green-colored popcorn in bags on St. Patrick's Day
- On Easter, they put up baby pictures of the executives and hold contests to "match" the executive to his or her childhood picture
- Low-fat frozen custard on the 4th of July
- A costume contest and pumpkin carving contest on Halloween
- A potluck brunch on Thanksgiving with each employee bringing in his or her favorite dish
- Holiday parties in December

- On each employee's birthday they receive three helium balloons on their door or their desk. Their birthday and company anniversary are published in the monthly employee calendar.

They even have a "File Clean Out Day" about twice a year where they encourage employees to do some "Spring cleaning." They bring in recycling bins and have contests for the most trash, the cleanest area, etc. Employees get to dress casually on that day. They also invite furniture representatives to show employees how to file, sit, and type in an ergonomically correct way.

> We act as though comfort and luxury were the chief requirements of life when all that we need to make us really happy is something to be enthusiastic about!
>
> **CHARLES KINGSLEY**

In some organizations with whom I've worked, senior executives spontaneously deliver treats to all the employees—ice cream bars, coffee and doughnuts, popcorn, candy bars, cupcakes—to celebrate sales successes or just to say "thanks!" To have a senior manager bring a treat to your desk definitely regenerates the spirit of caring!

Departments, divisions, or work teams can sponsor creative theme parties during lunch to appreciate their *internal* customers. Try a softball game, a picnic in the parking lot, an "old board games" party, or even an ethnic pot luck, inviting a different internal work group each month. Not only will spirit improve, but communication between groups will be enhanced and ultimately that will impact productivity.

TIPS FOR IMPLEMENTATION:

There is no limit to the creativity that can be generated in celebration. Just keep the issue of diversity in mind as you plan celebrations—make sure you acknowledge the holidays of all the religions and cultures represented in your workforce.

Work on a Community Project

THE IDEA:

Whenever you can work together as a team on a project bigger than your organization, you are creating a special spirit of sharing and caring.

THE IDEA IN ACTION:

 The city of Harlan, Iowa, my hometown, just completed a marvelous community project that involved local organizations and businesses, citizens, and even children. They built a "Dream Playground." This project was spearheaded by a single person, Mike Kolbe, the Advertising Manager for the Harlan Tribune, who made the dream playground come true. Everyone, regardless of age, was encouraged to come to work on it, and in the five days of building, over 600 people of all ages worked.

The playground was funded by donations from businesses and individuals and fund-raisers, including several run by the children of the community. In the "Coins for Kids" drive, they decorated collection cans and grocery sacks with pictures and "advertisements" for their new playground. These were used by the local stores to encourage people to make donations. And best of all, it is handicapped accessible.

> I think that what really separated us from stores like Culpepper's during our gestation period was our burning enthusiasm. There was a tangible sense of euphoria in every Body Shop. Maybe we were amateurs and, maybe we didn't look serious, but we were mad keen and excited by what was going on.
>
> **ANITA RODDICK**
> *The Body Shop*

TIPS FOR IMPLEMENTATION:

Some organizations participate in holiday projects to help others less fortunate in the community; others take on a project for Habitat for Humanity where they build houses for the homeless in their communities. What I particularly loved about the Iowa project was that they planned jobs for all ages—people with handyman or building skills built platforms, set poles, and put towers together; those with artistic talent created a replica of the Shelby County Courthouse; the children under age 10 were assigned jobs such as sanding boards, soaping screws, picking up scraps and garbage, and hauling gravel for the playground; those from 10 to 18 got to hammer, carry lumber, and work with the adults.

Mike said, "The community spirit was a joy to see! We got to work with people we've never known before. Lawyers, farmers, and young children worked right next to one another." In planning a project for your organization, consider one where every employee and perhaps even their families can be involved. And remember, this project only took one person with enthusiasm to get it started. Never ever give up your dream!

Make Every Friday or Saturday a Special Day

THE IDEA:

Since Fridays in most organizations seem interminable, it boosts spirit to make each Friday have a special theme. If your organization works on Saturdays, that is an even better time to regenerate spirit, since it is not a traditional work day and the mindset of most employees is that they shouldn't have to go to work since no one else does.

THE IDEA IN ACTION:

An organization with whom I've been working has decided to implement this idea in their offices on Saturdays. Here are some of the themes they've picked so far:

Green day

Weird games day

Hot dog day

Baby picture day

Crazy hat day

Bubble gum and comics day

Ice cream social day

Potluck Saturday

50s day

"Wanna Be" day

Dress like your favorite book/movie

Stripes day

TIPS FOR IMPLEMENTATION:

You may decide that once a month is enough activity to keep the spirit in your organization alive; however, I see how much employees enjoy and look forward to these events, and without a doubt, they contribute to happier employees and as a result, higher productivity. I suggest that after a few of these theme days, you spread out the responsibility. Perhaps one functional group or department or team can volunteer to plan a day. Or you may want to ask for volunteers to be a part of a task force for a short period of one to three months. The more involvement you have throughout the company, the more commitment there will be to continue. If you feel a theme day is too much, you may want to try having a special lunch theme once a week or once a month. Viscosity Oil in Willowbrook, Illinois, has work teams plan a lunch once a month with a theme and a budget. They have become very popular, and employees really look forward to them.

Create a Company Choir or Band

THE IDEA:

Help organize a group of people who love to sing into a company choir or those who play instruments into a company band. They can perform at company functions if they choose or just have a good time getting together and making music!

THE IDEA IN ACTION:

Jill Mallinder, the Manager of Education Services for the Switching Systems Division of Rockwell International in Downers Grove, Illinois, was "instrumental" in getting their company chorus started. It all began when employees sang a special "Rockwellized" version of the "12 Days of Christmas" at their annual Christmas party. Jill began talking about the idea and soon had someone volunteer to be the accompanist. A few weeks later, another person volunteered to be the director. They then posted recruitment signs all around the building, and today about 20 people show up every Wednesday at lunch to practice. They have even given their first company performance!

TIPS FOR IMPLEMENTATION:

An idea like this only needs an enthusiastic supporter to get it started. Could that cheerleader be YOU????

Draw a Vision of the Spirit in Your Workplace

THE IDEA:

Ask your colleagues to draw two pictures—one of what the spirit in their organization or department or team looks like *right now* and another of what they would like it to look like *in the future*. Then share these or post them in a breakout room.

THE IDEA IN ACTION:

I did this exercise with the training team of the Switching Systems Division of Rockwell International in Downers Grove, Illinois.

SPIRIT NOW: WHAT I'D LIKE IT TO BE:

One person drew a series of concentric circles, all separate and going in different directions. For the future he drew many curved intersecting lines, all intertwining at various points and all going towards the same end. Another person drew a bird physically struggling to sing, but the notes were blocked by many barriers. In the future she saw a beautiful bird effortlessly singing its song.

Someone else drew a picture of the present as a sea with many choppy waves, the sun almost hidden, and birds flying everywhere—some in the clouds, others caught in the waves, and still others going in many different directions. In her future view she drew a calm sea, a sun shining brightly, and all the birds flying in formation.

TIPS FOR IMPLEMENTATION:

This is a wonderful way for people to creatively and visually express their feelings about the present and then to create a vision for the future. Since most learners are visual, this exercise is particularly significant. It creates a sense of teamwork as they discuss what they have drawn, and the visions for the future draw them together in a new, creative spirit of hope.

Plan Special Holiday Activities

THE IDEA:

It always adds spirit to the workplace to celebrate holidays in special and fun ways.

THE IDEA IN ACTION:

Lands' End in Dodgeville, Wisconsin, plans an entire month of special activities in November and December:

Holiday Activity Calendar

Sunday	Monday	Tuesday	Wednesday	Thursday	Friday	Saturday
21	22 What is Harvey wearing?	23	24 Potluck Dress like a pilgrim	25 Thanksgiving Day!	26 Drawing for scavenger hunt.	27 Popcorn for the weekend in the Atrium
28 Popcorn for the weekend in the Atrium	29 <u>State Game Begins</u> Pick a seat ⟶	30	1 *December* To Win a⟶	2 Cookie / bar day bring a treat and share your recipe Gift--Certificate⟶	<u>Drawing for</u> <u>What's Harvey Wearing?ngwe</u> 3	4 (Seat assignments are used for GC drawing.)
5	State Game Drawing 6 <u>Family Tradition Week</u> Random⟶	7 Dress Goofy Day ___ Bingo Pick a seat ⟶	8 Christmas Jewelry Day ___ To Win	9 Fun Hat, Tie and Sock Day!	10 Wear Red, Green and Silver Day! _____	11 Popcorn in the Atrium
12 Popcorn in the Atrium	13 Random Drawing for Gift Certificate	14 Button Day	15 **Customer Sales Potluck**	16 Secret Pal Day Do something nice for a co-worker today!	17 Christmas Sweatshirt day ___ Button day	18 Popcorn in the Atrium
19 Popcorn in the Atrium	20	21 **Wear your Holiday Best Day!**	22 Secret Pal Day Do something nice for a co-worker today!	23	24 **Christmas Eve**	25 **Christmas Day**

They also use a bulletin board to display family holiday traditions submitted by the employees.

TIPS FOR IMPLEMENTATION:

One of the keys to having successful activities is to get employees involved. Lands' End has employee-run committees that plan, communicate, and accomplish monthly activities. Some committees are: Birthday committee (sign cards each month for the current birthdays and post the monthly birthday list); Social committee (plan monthly fun events such as order Bingo, scavenger hunts, theme dress-up days, potlucks, ice cream days, etc.); Bulletin board committee (keep bulletin boards current, post relevant material); WOW (facilitate the WOW program to appreciate others).

Sponsor Fun Contests

THE IDEA:

Get your creative juices going and sponsor exciting and fun contests that will delight internal and external customers alike.

THE IDEA IN ACTION:

 Lands' End in Dodgeville, Wisconsin, has some wonderful contests to keep its telephone reps on their toes.

> Baseball—Any orders taken from or shipped to cities of major leagues gives the team a base hit. They need 20 different order numbers to fill all the bases, and they can have a total of five runs per sheet. The winning team is the one that fills the most sheets.

> Stars and Stripes—Take orders from all 50 states and fill in the stars; find the words "Clinton, Gore, Hillary, Kennedy, Carter, Nixon, and Bush" and place the order number on a stripe on the flag. Fill as many sheets as you can.

> Nice Call, Nasty Call—For a nice call, both the caller and the rep who handled the call receive a gift certificate. For a nasty call, the customer gets deleted from the mailing list, and the rep receives a gift certificate. They have fun with this one at Christmas.

Some of the prizes they award are a $5 gift certificate from Lands' End; a $5 gift certificate from a local business; Start 15 minutes late on one shift; One additional 15 minute break; A 45-minute lunch without adjusting; Leave 15 minutes early one shift; Pick your shift on a day when you are scheduled to work; A day to have the seat of your choice. Diane Smith Hole, the Manager of Training says, "We spend about $20 on prizes for activities. The reps enjoy small prizes like candy bars and M&M's since the price is low and more can win."

TIPS FOR IMPLEMENTATION:

It is most fun if you make the contest a memorable one, tying it to a holiday, or doing something that is different from the ordinary contests we all experience.

Get a Company or Department Mascot

THE IDEA:

Decide as a company or a department what would make the best mascot for your group and have fun with your choice.

THE IDEA IN ACTION:

Rosenbluth Travel in Philadelphia uses a salmon for its mascot because "they are always swimming upstream." They give out stuffed animal salmon and chocolate salmon for gifts to customers, salmon pins for rewards for employees, and even salmon note cards and stickers.[1]

When I came to Enterprise Systems in Wheeling, Illinois, to do a presentation, one of the first things I noticed was the following sign posted all over the building: **FROG MISSING—REWARD!**

During the day, various ransom messages and replies were read over the PA system. When I asked about this, I was told that no one knew what had happened, but the marketing frog was missing! After some lengthy research, I received an anonymous letter from the notorious "Frognapper" describing how this all came about.

The Frognapping Caper

The new Marketing Director, Kathy Sharo, brought with her an eight-inch ceramic frog that she made into the department mascot. This frog would travel from one individual's desk to another within the department, sit there for a few days and then move to another. One day I was just walking by when I

"They started me out in obedience school. I liked It so much I put myself through college, got an MBA and replaced my master at work."

spotted the frog and for no particular reason decided to take it for a walk. Since no one saw me traveling through the halls with it, I eventually brought it into my office and decided to hide it. Once hidden, the next logical step was to have some fun with the situation.

And so began the ransom notes! These notes were anonymously delivered by typing them into my computer and then printing them off at a centrally located printer. Each ransom note had the heading, "Please deliver to Michele Boeding," the individual who last had the frog on her desk. By creating the

ransom notes in this manner, no one knew who the culprit was!
There were many notes:

#1 Unless you meet our demands, the frog is a croaker!

#2 During negotiations of ransom
always seek opportunities that sum
information in the shape of clues
saves froggie from simmering in stu
(Each ransom note had two misspelled words that were clues)

#3 Like the mellow paced turtle
and the sure-footed hair
rewards will get you diddle
while ransom pays her fair
(This was in response to a "reward for information" poster
that Michele created trying to get the frog back).

#4 We repeatedly have tried to make the damn frog sing
by threatening hands around her neck "that would ring"
but she wouldn't spill marketing's plans, thus we failed
so ransom is on it's way posted internal male

This little charade has been fun
but unfortunately it is done
the culprits you will seek
are we wise, wild, or meek?
this mystery now you must tweak.
(This note was left upon the frog's
return.)

It was the talk of the office for a
few days with a lot of potential
suspects, but the real culprit was
never found. And so it remains an
Enterprise mystery . . .

TIPS FOR IMPLEMENTATION:

Just think of how many ways a mascot
can boost company spirit! Have fun
choosing one in your place of work.

> **The passions are the only advocates which always persuade. The simplest man with passion will be more persuasive than the most eloquent without.**
>
> **LaRochefoucauld,**
> *17th Century*
> *French Philosopher*

"So I said, "Listen, clown...", oh, hi Ed."

Try Something New Each Week

THE IDEA:

To keep your own spirits high and your creative juices going, try at least one new thing each week.

THE IDEA IN ACTION:

Tom Peters suggests that each week you eat lunch with one new person in your organization. Most of us eat lunch with the same people every day, so we don't get to know others who may work in different parts of the building. Just go through the employee directory and call someone up and ask them to have lunch with you one day that week. You'll be amazed at how your network will increase!

Some other suggestions are to try a different route to work one day a week or take your break at a different time once a week or go for a long walk instead of spending your full lunch hour in the cafeteria. Read a new periodical every week—think of how many new magazines and newsletters you could evaluate if you just read one new one a week!

Gloria Runk, the Assistant Manager of the Citicorp Worldwide Security Services Training Department in Tampa, Florida, says:
Every day I resolve to:

1. Do something for someone else.

2. Do something for myself.

3. Do something I don't want to do that needs doing.

4. Do a physical exercise.

5. Do a mental exercise.

6. Do something that creates humor.

7. Do an original prayer that always includes counting my blessings.

TIPS FOR IMPLEMENTATION:

I have found that it is important to have a strategy when you begin something new, at least until that new behavior becomes a habit and there is less likelihood of your forgetting to do it. My personal strategy for trying something new each week is that I always do it on Thursday. That way I can check myself, and I am more likely to remember my commitment.

Notes

1. Rosenbluth, Hal & McFerrin, Diane. 1992. *The Customer Comes Second*, New York, NY: William Morrow and Company, Inc.

Personal Action Ideas

Write your ideas here!

SUMMARY

Life is no brief candle to me. It is a sort of splendid torch which I have got hold of for the moment, and I want to make it burn as brightly as possible before handing it on to future generations.

GEORGE BERNARD SHAW

You CAN Make a Difference!

Far away there in the sunshine are my highest aspirations. I may not reach them, but I can look up and see their beauty, believe in them and try to follow where they lead.

LOUISA MAY ALCOTT

Anita Roddick of the Body Shop, definitely a spirited place to work, states these three things as her corporate vision and values:

1. First, you have to have fun
2. Second, you have to put love where your labour is.
3. Third you have to go in the opposite direction to everyone else.[1]

Fun is demonstrated through Atmosphere, Appreciation for All, and Enthusiasm. Love is exemplified by Empathy, Respect, and Reason for Being.

Going in the opposite direction is Creativity. She has incorporated all the elements of a spirited workplace to achieve unheard of success in the retail profession. You can have that success, too, as you apply the ideas in this book.

Spirit in the workplace begins with the individual and spreads to the team. When I spoke last fall on "Regenerating the Spirit in your Workplace" to Sprint Cellular's Customer Service Managers, one of the evaluations said, "If each attendee puts one idea to work, we can make a tremendous difference—both for the company and for each individual associate." Let that new spirit begin with you.

> One thing I know; the only ones among you who will be truly happy are those who will have sought and found how to serve.
>
> **ALBERT SCHWEITZER**

David Noer, a vice president for the Center for Creative Leadership, says, "Think of it as a wonderful wakeup call, to apply your human spirit to the world of work, to do something besides making other people wealthy, to make a real difference in this world."[2] And Lawrence Perlman, CEO of Minneapolis-based Ceridian Corporation says, "Ultimately, the combination of head and heart will be a competitive advantage."[3]

> Allow who you are on the inside to be who you are on the outside.
>
> **ANONYMOUS**

Imagine a place of work where employees put the needs of others first and where respect for one another abounds; where caring and appreciation permeate the atmosphere; where there is open communciation and where creativity is rampant; where there is laughter and where people are committed to making a difference through their interactions and their very important work; and where there is excitement and enthusiasm even in daily tasks. That is the workplace you can begin to create wherever you are.

> It's easy to make a buck. It's a lot tougher to make a difference.
>
> **TOM BROKAW**

Finally, I want to share with you RULE TEN from my friend Og Mandino's beautiful book A *Better Way to Live* (1991) as a guide for the way you, as one individual, can begin to regenerate spirit in your own place of work:

Beginning today, treat everyone you meet, friend or foe, loved one or stranger, as if they were going to be dead at midnight. Extend to each person, no matter how trivial the contact, all the care and kindness and understanding and love that you can muster, and do it with no thought of any reward. Your life will never be the same again.

You CAN make a difference!

Notes

1. Roddick, Anita. 1991. *Body and Soul*, New York, NY: Crown Trade Paperbacks, p. 128.
2. Miller Rubin, Bonnie. 1995. "The Death of Ambition." *Chicago Tribune Magazine*, 22 January, p. 15.
3. Galen, Michele & West, Karen. 1995. "Companies Hit the Road Less Traveled." *Business Week*, 5 June, pp. 82–84.

List of Persons to Whom I Will Send CARE Packages

Ideas I Will Apply in My Work Group

MORE CARE PACKAGES! 🎁 🎁 🎁 🎁 🎁

If you have stories of heart-warming care packages from your workplace, please send them to me! I would like to include them in a future edition of this book. Include the names of the company and everyone involved, so I can credit them where appropriate.

Barbara Glanz
More Care Packages
4047 Howard Avenue
Western Springs, IL 60558
fax: 708-246-5123
tel: 708-246-8594

RESOURCES:

About the Artist

Rita Blitt
8900 State Line, Suite 333
Leawood, KS 66206
913-381-3840

Rita Blitt, Leawood, Kansas, is an internationally recognized painter/sculptor. Her works are exhibited in parks, malls, public buildings, museums, and galleries around the world. *Joie de vivre* leaps from her work on paper, canvas, and in wood, acrylic, and metal. I am thrilled to have original drawings from Rita in this book. Her very special spirit is a gift to us all.

The HUMOR Project
Joel Goodman, President
110 Spring Street
Saratoga Springs, New York 12866-3397
518-587-8770
Fax 518-587-8771

The Humor Project publishes "Laughing Matters" magazine, a catalog of HUMOResources, and sponsors annually The International Conference on The Positive Power of Humor and Creativity.

David Roth
Maythelight Music
18952—40th Place NE
Seattle, WA 98155-2810
Contact him for information on other CDs and tapes.
To order a video of "A Little Something More" (The Johnny Story song) by David Roth, send $20 (NY residents add sales tax) plus $2 shipping/handling to:
HVN Productions
P.O. Box 3065
Ronkonkoma, NY 11779
1-615-588-1798

To order any of the "Kindness is Contagious...Catch It!" products (buttons, posters, bumper stickers, program guide booklets, T-shirts), contact:
Stop Violence Coalition
301 E. Armour, Suite 205
Kansas City, MO 64111
816-753-8022; 816-753-8056 FAX

Blanchard Training and Development
World Headquarters
125 State Place
Escondido, CA 92029-1398
619-489-5005; 800-728-6000

Hyler Bracey
The Atlanta Consulting Group
2028 Powers Ferry Road
Suite 190
Atlanta, GA 30339
404-952-8000

Successories (motivational materials and rewards)
919 Springer Drive
Lombard, Illinois 60148
1-800-621-1423, Ext. 5105

Mike Kolbe (**Dream Playground** Organizer)
Harlan Tribune Newspapers
Harlan, Iowa
Work: 712-755-3111
Fax: 712-755-3324
Home: 712-755-5546

The "Red Plate"
Waechtersbach USA
4201 N.E. 34th Street
Kansas City, Missouri 64117
816-455-3800
Fax: 816-459-7705

Train Reinforce, and Inspire (motivational material and rewards)
650 West Grand Avenue, Suite 102
Elmhurst, Illinois 60126-1061
1-800-993-6399
Fax: 708-993-9932

Bill McAlpine, Cartoonist
McToons
1280 Spaulding Road
Bartlett, Illinois
708-837-4679

Bonnie Michaels, President
Managing Work & Family
912 Crain Street
Evanston, Illinois 60202
708-864-0916
Fax: 708-475-2021

Where Did the First CARE Package® Come From

In the process of researching this book, I learned about the wonderful history of the care package, which originated with CARE, the international relief and development agency. I'd like to share this story with you.

On a sunny afternoon, in May 1946, a small crowd formed on the docks of Le Havre, a French city still in ruins from the war. A local resistance hero, Marcel Fernez, stepped through the gathering of friends and neighbors to sign for a food parcel sent to him by an American he had never met. As he hoisted the parcel up onto his shoulder, Fernez became the recipient of the very first CARE Package®. This plain brown package of food was the creation of a new American charity—CARE—founded to help survivors of World War II. In the years that followed, Americans sent some 100 million CARE Packages to people in need all over the world; and CARE continues to help the world's poor today.

CARE® (which stands for "Cooperative for Assistance and Relief Everywhere") still provides people with the ability to touch lives and make a difference. Several of CARE's current donors are people who have become self-sufficient through CARE programs and want to give others the same opportunity. This spirit has helped make CARE the world's largest relief and development agency in existence today, and it literally thrives on the unconditional caring felt by Americans that transcends politics, race, nationality, and all other barriers separating people.

CARE continues its mission of working with the world's needy and giving them the tools to achieve economic and social well-being. CARE now works with 48 million people in 66 developing and emerging nations in Africa, Asia, Eastern Europe, and Latin America. Its programs encompass health, nutrition, family planning, emergency relief, girls education, small business support, agriculture, and environmental protection. And 50 years after the first CARE Package arrived in France, CARE has returned to Europe to assist the people of Bosnia recovering from war and ethnic strife.

Over its 50-year history, CARE has brought its message of hope to more than one billion people in 125 countries. For more information about CARE, please see the organization's site on the World Wide Webb at www.care.org. Or contact: 151 Ellis Street, Atlanta, GA 30303; 800-422-7385; or info@care.org.

CARE and CARE Package are registered service marks of the Cooperative for Assistance and Relief Everywhere, Inc.

BIBLIOGRAPHY:

C = Creative Communication

Albrecht, Karl. 1987. *The Creative Corporation*. Burr Ridge, IL: Irwin Professional Publishing.

Buzan, Tony. 1983. *Use Both Sides of your Brain*. New York, NY: E. P. Dutton.

Campbell, Ph.D., David. 1977. *Take the Road to Creativity and Get Off your Dead End*. Greensboro, NC: Center for Creative Leadership.

Glanz, Barbara. 1993. *The Creative Communicator—399 Tools to Communicate Commitment without Boring People to Death!* Burr Ridge, IL: Irwin Professional Publishing.

Herrmann, Ned. 1988. *The Creative Brain*. Lake Lure, NC: Brain Books.

Michalko, Michael. 1991. *Thinkertoys*. Berkeley, CA: Ten Speed Press.

Ray, Michael & Myers, Rochelle. 1986. *Creativity in Business*. New York, NY: Doubleday.

Rosenbluth, Hal & McFerrin Peters, Diane. 1992. *The Customer Comes Second*. New York, NY: William Morrow and Co., Inc.

von Oech, Roger. 1990. *A Whack on the Side of the Head*. New York, NY: Warner Books, Inc.

A = Atmosphere and Appreciation for All

Canfield, Jack & Victor Hansen, Mark. 1993. *Chicken Soup for the Soul*. Deerfield Beach, FL: Health Communications, Inc.

Editors of Conari Press. 1993. *Random Acts of Kindness*. Berkeley, CA: Conari Press.

Garfield, Charles. 1992. *Second to None: How Our Smartest Companies Put People First*. Burr Ridge, IL: Irwin Professional Publishing.

Glanz, Barbara. 1993. *The Creative Communicator—399 Tools to Communicate Commitment without Boring People to Death!* Burr Ridge, IL: Irwin Professional Publishing.

Goodman, Joel. 1995. *Laffirmations—1001 Ways to Add Humor to Your Life and Work*. Deerfield Beach, FL: Health Communications, Inc.

Le Boeuf, Michael. 1985. *The Greatest Management Principle in the World*. New York, NY: G.P. Putnam's Sons, Inc.

Levering, Robert. 1988. *A Great Place to Work*. New York, NY: Random House.

Liebig, James E. 1991. *Business Ethics—Profiles in Civic Virtue*. Golden, CO: Fulcrum.

Nelson, Bob. 1994. *1001 Ways to Reward Employees*. New York, NY: Workman Publishing.

R = Respect and Reason for Being

Block, Peter. 1993. *Stewardship—Choosing Service Over Self-Interest*. San Francisco, CA: Berrett Koehler.

Covey, Stephen. 1991. *Principle-Centered Leadership*. New York, NY: Summit.

De Pree, Max. 1989. *Leadership Is an Art*. New York, NY: Doubleday.

De Pree, Max. 1992. *Leadership Jazz*. New York, NY: Doubleday Currency.

Garfield, Charles. 1986. *Peak Performers*. New York, NY: William Morrow and Co., Inc.

Harvey, Eric & Lucia, Al. 1993. *Walk the Talk*. Dallas, TX: Performance Systems, Inc.

Lindbergh, Anne Morrow. 1975. *Gift from the Sea*. New York, NY: Pantheon Books.

Mandino, Og. 1991. A *Better Way to Live*. New York, NY: Bantam Books.

Manning, Curtis & Mcmillen. 1996. *Building Community—The Human Side of Work*. Cincinnati, OH: Thomson Executive Press.

McCann, Ron & Vitale, Joe. 1989. *The Joy of Service*. Stafford, TX: Service Information Source Publications.

McGee-Cooper, Ann. 1992. *You Don't Have to Go Home from Work Exhausted*. New York, NY: Bantam Books.

Oakley, Ed & Krug, Doug. 1991. *Enlightened Leadership*. Denver, CO: Stonetree.

Siegel, Bernie S., M.D. 1989. *Peace, Love, and Healing*. New York, NY: Harper & Row.

▬ E ▬ Empathy and Enthusiasm

American Media. 1992. "Good Enough Isn't Good Enough" Videotape. American Media: Des Moines, IA.

Autry, James A. 1991. *Love and Profit—The Art of Caring Leadership*. New York, NY: Morrow.

Bracey, Hyler; Rosenblum, Jack; Sanford, Aubrey & Trueblood, Roy. 1990. *Managing from the Heart*. Heart Enterprises: Atlanta, GA.

Cannon, Janell. 1993. *Stellaluna*. San Diego: Harcourt Brace and Co.

Covey, Stephen. 1989. *The Seven Habits of Highly Effective People*. New York, NY: Simon and Schuster.

DeAngelis, Ph.D., Barbara. 1994. *Real Moments*. New York, NY: Delacorte Press.

Johnson, Barbara. 1992. *Splashes of Joy in the Cesspools of Life*. Dallas, TX: Word Publishing.

Mandino, Og. 1991. A *Better Way to Live*. New York, NY: Bantam Books.

Rind, David. 1993. "Triumph Over Odds," Videotape V93-3. Dallas, TX: 1993 National Speaker's Association 20th Annual Convention; Palm Desert, CA: Convention Cassettes Unlimited.

Robbins, Anthony. 1991. *Unlimited Power*. New York, NY: Bradbury Press.

ABOUT BARBARA GLANZ

Barbara Glanz is an internationally known author, speaker, and consultant and the president of Barbara Glanz Communications, Inc., in Western Springs, Illinois. She specializes in three areas: Creative Communication, Building Customer Loyalty, and Regenerating the Spirit in the Workplace. She has spoken on three continents, and her books have been featured in *Entrepreneur* magazine, the *Chicago Tribune*, *Executive Female* magazine, "The Service Edge," and "Communication Briefings."

Known as the business speaker who speaks to your heart as well as to your head, Barbara is the author of *The Creative Communicator—399 Tools to Communicate Commitment without Boring People to Death!*, and *Building Customer Loyalty—How YOU Can Help Keep Customers Returning*.

Since 1987 Barbara has trained thousands of people in North America and has spoken worldwide to conferences, associations, government organizations, and companies both large and small. Some of her clients include: Abbott Labs, Rockwell International, Sprint Cellular, Mobil Research and Development Corporation, First Chicago Bank, Blue Cross Blue Shield, IBM, AT&T, the New Zealand Institute of Travel and Tourism, Southwest Airlines, Hawaiian Electric Company, Nationwide Insurance, USAA, APAC TeleServices, Hilton Hotels, Kroger Company, Bank of Montreal, the State of Michigan, the Hellenic Management Association, the Foreign Missions Board, and the Ohio Department of Development.